The Maid of Honour by Philip Massinger

Philip Massinger was baptized at St. Thomas's in Salisbury on November 24th, 1583.

Massinger is described in his matriculation entry at St. Alban Hall, Oxford (1602), as the son of a gentleman. His father, who had also been educated there, was a member of parliament, and attached to the household of Henry Herbert, 2nd Earl of Pembroke. The Earl was later seen as a potential patron for Massinger.

He left Oxford in 1606 without a degree. His father had died in 1603, and accounts suggest that Massinger was left with no financial support this, together with rumours that he had converted to Catholicism, meant the next stage of his career needed to provide an income.

Massinger went to London to make his living as a dramatist, but he is only recorded as author some fifteen years later, when The Virgin Martyr (1621) is given as the work of Massinger and Thomas Dekker.

During those early years as a playwright he wrote for the Elizabethan stage entrepreneur, Philip Henslowe. It was a difficult existence. Poverty was always close and there was constant pleading for advance payments on forthcoming works merely to survive.

After Henslowe died in 1616 Massinger and John Fletcher began to write primarily for the King's Men and Massinger would write regularly for them until his death.

The tone of the dedications in later plays suggests evidence of his continued poverty. In the preface of The Maid of Honour (1632) he wrote, addressing Sir Francis Foljambe and Sir Thomas Bland: "I had not to this time subsisted, but that I was supported by your frequent courtesies and favours."

The prologue to The Guardian (1633) refers to two unsuccessful plays and two years of silence, when the author feared he had lost popular favour although, from the little evidence that survives, it also seems he had involved some of his plays with political characters which would have cast shadows upon England's alliances.

Philip Massinger died suddenly at his house near the Globe Theatre on March 17th, 1640. He was buried the next day in the churchyard of St. Saviour's, Southwark, on March 18th, 1640. In the entry in the parish register he is described as a "stranger," which, however, implies nothing more than that he belonged to another parish.

Index of Contents

INTRODUCTION

This tragi-comedy, which was first printed in 1632, was, as the old title-page informs us, very frequently acted "at the Phoenix in Drury-lane, by the Queen's Majesty's servants." It was a great favourite, and with justice, for it has a thousand claims to admiration, and is of the higher order of Massinger's plays. It will not, indeed, be very easy to find in any writer a subject more animated, or characters more variously and pointedly drawn. There is no delay in introducing the business of the drama; and nothing is allowed to interfere with its progress. Indeed this is by far too rapid; and event is precipitated upon event without regard to time or place. But Massinger acts with a liberty which it would be absurd to criticise. Thebes and Athens, Palermo and Sienna, are alike to him; and he must be allowed to transport his agents and their concerns from one to another, as often as the exigencies of his ambulatory plan may require.

It is observable, that in this play Massinger has attempted the more difficult part of dramatic writing. He is not content with describing different qualities in his characters; but lays before the reader several differences of the same qualities. The courage of Gonzaga, though by no means inferior to it, is not that of Bertoldo. In the former, it is a fixed and habitual principle, the honourable business of his life. In the latter, it is an irresistible impulse, the instantaneous result of a fiery temper. There is still another remove; and these branches of real courage differ from the poor and forced approaches to valour in Gasparo and Antonio. A broader distinction is used with his two courtiers; and the cold interest of Astutio is fully contrasted with the dazzling and imprudent assumption of Fulgentio. But Camiola herself is the great object that reigns throughout the piece. Every where she animates us with her spirit, and instructs us with her sense. Yet this superiority takes nothing from her softer feelings. Her tears flow with a mingled fondness and regret; and she is swayed by a passion which is only quelled by her greater resolution. The influence of her character is also heightened through the different manner of her lovers; through the mad impatience of the uncontrolled Bertoldo, the glittering pretensions of Fulgentio, and the humble and sincere attachment of Adorni, who nourishes secret desires of a happiness too exalted for him, faithfully performs commands prejudicial to his own views, through the force of an affection which ensures his obedience, and, amidst so much service, scarcely presumes to hint the passion which consumes him. I know not if even signior Sylli is wholly useless here; he serves at least to show her good-humoured toleration of a being hardly important enough for her contempt.

In the midst of this just praise of Camiola, there are a few things to be regretted. Reason and religion had forbidden her union with Bertoldo; and she had declared herself unalterable in her purpose. His captivity reverses her judgment, and she determines not only to liberate, but to marry him. Unfortunately too she demands a sealed contract as the condition of his freedom; though Bertoldo's ardour was already known to her, and the generosity of her nature ought to have abstained from so degrading a bargain. But Massinger wanted to hinder the marriage of Aurelia; and, with an infelicity which attends many of his contrivances, he provided a prior contract at the expense of the delicacy, as well as the principles of his heroine. It is well, that the nobleness of the conclusion throws the veil over these blemishes. Her determination is at once natural and unexpected. It answers to the original independence of her character, and she retires with our highest admiration and esteem.

It may be observed here, that Massinger was not unknown to Milton. The date of some of Milton's early poems, indeed, is not exactly ascertained; but if the reader will compare the speech of Paulo, with the Penseroso, he cannot fail to remark a similarity in the cadences, as well as in the measure and the solemnity of the thoughts.

On many other occasions he certainly remembers Massinger, and frequently in his representations of female purity, and the commanding dignity of virtue.

A noble lesson arises from the conduct of the principal character. A fixed sense of truth and rectitude gives genuine superiority; it corrects the proud, and abashes the vain, and marks the proper limits between humility and presumption. It also governs itself with the same ascendancy which it establishes over others. When the lawful objects of life cannot be possessed with clearness of honour, it provides a nobler pleasure in rising above their attraction, and creates a new happiness by controlling even innocent desires.

TO MY MOST HONOURED FRIENDS, SIR FRANCIS FOLJAMBE, KNT. AND BART. AND SIR THOMAS BLAND, KNT.

That you have been, and continued so for many years, since you vouchsafed to own me, patrons to me and my despised studies, I cannot but with all humble thankfulness acknowledge: and living, as you have done, inseparable in your friendship, (notwithstanding all differences, and suits in law arising between you[1],) I held it as impertinent as absurd, in the presentment of my service in this kind, to divide you. A free confession of a debt, in a meaner man, is the amplest satisfaction to his superiors; and I heartily wish that the world may take notice, and from myself, that I had not to this time subsisted, but that I was supported by your frequent courtesies and favours. When your more serious occasions will give you leave, you may please to peruse this trifle, and peradventure find something in it that may appear worthy of your protection. Receive it, I beseech you, as a testimony of his duty who, while he lives, resolves to be truly and sincerely devoted to your service,

PHILIP MASSINGER.

FOOTNOTE

[1] Notwithstanding all differences, and suits in late arising between you.] The suits in law subsisting between these fast friends of Massinger—Sir Francis Foljambe, of Walton, in the county of Derby, and Sir Thomas Bland, of Kippax Park, in the county of York—originated in a question as to the right of working some coal-mines.—GILCHRIST.

DRAMATIS PERSONÆ

ROBERTO, king of Sicily.
FERDINAND, duke of Urbin.
BERTOLDO, the king's natural brother, a knight of Malta.
GONZAGA, a knight of Malta, general to the duchess of Sienna.
ASTUTIO, a counsellor of state.
FULGENTIO, the minion of ROBERTO.
ADORNI, a follower of CAMIOLA'S father.
SIGNIOR SYLLI, a foolish self-lover.
ANTONIO,   }
GASPARO,   } two rich heirs, city-bred.
PIERIO, a colonel to GONZAGA.
RODERIGO,   }
JACOMO,   } captains to GONZAGA.
DRUSO,   }
LIVIO,   } captains to duke FERDINAND.
Father PAULO, a priest, CAMIOLA's confessor.
Ambassador from the duke of Urbin.
A Bishop.
A Page.

AURELIA, duchess of Sienna.
CAMIOLA, the Maid of Honour.
CLARINDA, her woman.

Scout, Soldiers, Gaoler, Attendants, Servants, &c.

SCENE - Partly in Sicily, and partly in the Siennese.

THE MAID OF HONOUR

Enter **ASTUTIO** and **ADORNI**.

ADORNI
Good day to your lordship.

ASTUTIO
Thanks, Adorni.

ADORNI
May I presume to ask if the ambassador
Employ'd by Ferdinand, the duke of Urbin,
Hath audience this morning?

[Enter **FULGENTIO**.

ASTUTIO
'Tis uncertain;
For, though a counsellor of state, I am not
Of the cabinet council: but there's one, if he please,
That may resolve you.

ADORNI
I will move him.—Sir!

FULGENTIO
If you've a suit, show water[1], I am blind else.

ADORNI
A suit; yet of a nature not to prove
The quarry[2] that you hawk for: if your words
Are not like Indian wares, and every scruple
To be weigh'd and rated, one poor syllable,
Vouchsafed in answer of a fair demand,
Cannot deserve a fee.

FULGENTIO
It seems you are ignorant,
I neither speak nor hold my peace for nothing;
And yet, for once, I care not if I answer
One single question, gratis.

ADORNI

I much thank you.
Hath the ambassador audience, sir, to-day?

FULGENTIO
Yes.

ADORNI
At what hour?

FULGENTIO
I promised not so much.
A syllable you begg'd, my charity gave it;
Move me no further.

[Exit.

ASTUTIO
This you wonder at:
With me, 'tis usual.

ADORNI
Pray you, sir, what is he?

ASTUTIO
No gentleman, yet a lord. He hath some drops
Of the king's blood running in his veins, derived
Some ten degrees off. His revenue lies
In a narrow compass, the king's ear; and yields him
Every hour a fruitful harvest. Men may talk
Of three crops in a year in the Fortunate Islands,
Or profit made by wool; but, while there are suitors,
His sheepshearing, nay, shaving to the quick,
Is in every quarter of the moon, and constant.
In the time of trussing a point,[3] he can undo,
Or make a man: his play or recreation,
Is to raise this up, or pull down that; and, though
He never yet took orders, makes more bishops
In Sicily, than the pope himself.

[Enter **BERTOLDO, GASPARO, ANTONIO**, and a **SERVANT**.

ADORNI
Most strange!

ASTUTIO
The presence fills. He in the Malta habit[4]
Is the king's natural brother.

ADORNI
I understand you.

BERTOLDO
With this jewel
Presented to Camiola, prepare,
This night, a visit for me.

[Exit **SERVANT**.]

I shall have
Your company, gallants, I perceive, if that
The king will hear of war.

ANTONIO
You are, sir,
A knight of Malta, and, as I have heard,
Have served against the Turk.

BERTOLDO
'Tis true.

ANTONIO
Pray you, show us
The difference between the city valour,
And service in the field.

BERTOLDO
'Tis somewhat more
Than roaring in a tavern or a brothel,
Or to steal a constable[5] from a sleeping watch,
Then burn their halberds; or, safe guarded by
Your tenant's sons, to carry away a May-pole
From a neighbour village. You will not find there
Your masters of dependencies[6] to take up
A drunken brawl, or, to get you the names
Of valiant chevaliers, fellows that will be,
For a cloak with thrice-dyed velvet, and a cast suit,
Kick'd down the stairs. A knave with a provant sword[7],
If you bear not yourself both in and upright,
Will slash your scarlets and your plush a new way;
Or, with the hilts, thunder about your ears
Such music as will make your worships dance
To the doleful tune of Lachrymæ[8].

GASPARO
I must tell you
In private, as you are my princely friend,

I do not like such fiddlers.

BERTOLDO
No! they are useful
For your imitation; I remember you,
When you came first to the court, and talk'd of nothing
But your rents and your entradas[9], ever chiming
The golden bells in your pockets; you believed
The taking of the wall as a tribute due to
Your gaudy clothes; and could not walk at midnight
Without a causeless quarrel, as if men
Of coarser outsides were in duty bound
To suffer your affronts: but, when you had been
Cudgell'd well twice or thrice, and from the doctrine
Made profitable uses, you concluded,
The sovereign means to teach irregular heirs
Civility, with conformity of manners,
Were two or three sound beatings.

ANTONIO
I confess
They did much good upon me.

GASPARO
And on me:
The principles that they read were sound.

BERTOLDO
You'll find
The like instructions in the camp.

ASTUTIO
The king!

[A flourish. Enter **ROBERTO, FULGENTIO, AMBASSADOR,** and **ATTENDANTS.**

ROBERTO [Ascends the throne.]
We sit prepared to hear.

AMBASSADOR
Your majesty
Hath been long since familiar, I doubt not,
With the desperate fortunes of my lord; and pity
Of the much that your confederate hath suffer'd,
You being his last refuge, may persuade you
Not alone to compassionate, but to lend
Your royal aids to stay him in his fall
To certain ruin. He, too late, is conscious

That his ambition to encroach upon
His neighbour's territories, with the danger of
His liberty, nay, his life, hath brought in question
His own inheritance: but youth, and heat
Of blood, in your interpretation, may
Both plead and mediate for him. I must grant it
An error in him, being denied the favours
Of the fair princess of Sienna, (though
He sought her in a noble way,) to endeavour
To force affection by surprisal of
Her principal seat, Sienna.

ROBERTO
Which now proves
The seat of his captivity, not triumph:
Heaven is still just.

AMBASSADOR
And yet that justice is
To be with mercy temper'd, which heaven's deputies
Stand bound to minister. The injured duchess,
By reason taught, as nature, could not, with
The reparation of her wrongs, but aim at
A brave revenge; and my lord feels, too late,
That innocence will find friends. The great Gonzaga,
The honour of his order, (I must praise
Virtue, though in an enemy,) he whose fights
And conquests hold one number, rallying up
Her scatter'd troops, before we could get time
To victual or to man the conquer'd city,
Sat down before it; and presuming that
'Tis not to be relieved, admits no parley,
Our flags of truce hung out in vain: nor will he
Lend an ear to composition, but exacts,
With the rendering up the town, the goods and lives
Of all within the walls, and of all sexes,
To be at his discretion.

ROBERTO
Since injustice
In your duke meets this correction, can you press us,
With any seeming argument of reason,
In foolish pity to decline[10] his dangers,
To draw them on ourself? Shall we not be
Warn'd by his harms? The league proclaim'd between us
Bound neither of us further than to aid
Each other, if by foreign force invaded;
And so far in my honour I was tied.

But since, without our counsel, or allowance,
He hath ta'en arms; with his good leave, he must
Excuse us if we steer not on a rock
We see, and may avoid. Let other monarchs
Contend to be made glorious by proud war,
And, with the blood of their poor subjects, purchase
Increase of empire, and augment their cares
In keeping that which was by wrongs extorted,
Gilding unjust invasions with the trim
Of glorious conquests; we, that would be known
The father of our people, in our study
And vigilance for their safety, must not change
Their ploughshares into swords, and force them from
The secure shade of their own vines, to be
Scorch'd with the flames of war; or, for our sport,
Expose their lives to ruin.

AMBASSADOR
Will you, then,
In his extremity, forsake your friend?

ROBERTO
No; but preserve ourself.

BERTOLDO
Cannot the beams
Of honour thaw your icy fears?

ROBERTO
Who's that?

BERTOLDO
A kind of brother, sir, howe'er your subject;
Your father's son, and one who blushes that
You are not heir to his brave spirit and vigour,
As to his kingdom.

ROBERTO
How's this!

BERTOLDO
Sir, to be
His living chronicle, and to speak his praise,
Cannot deserve your anger.

ROBERTO
Where's your warrant
For this presumption?

BERTOLDO
Here, sir, in my heart:
Let sycophants, that feed upon your favours,
Style coldness in you caution, and prefer
Your ease before your honour; and conclude,
To eat and sleep supinely is the end
Of human blessings: I must tell you, sir,
Virtue, if not in action, is a vice;
And when we move not forward, we go backward[11]:
Nor is this peace, the nurse of drones and cowards,
Our health, but a disease.

GASPARO
Well urged, my lord.

ANTONIO
Perfect what is so well begun.

AMBASSADOR
And bind
My lord your servant.

ROBERTO
Hair-brain'd fool! what reason
Canst thou infer, to make this good?

BERTOLDO
A thousand,
Not to be contradicted. But consider
Where your command lies: 'tis not, sir, in France,
Spain, Germany, Portugal, but in Sicily;
An island, sir. Here are no mines of gold
Or silver to enrich you; no worm spins
Silk in her womb, to make distinction
Between you and a peasant, in your habits;
No fish lives near our shores, whose blood can dye
Scarlet or purple; all that we possess,
With beasts we have in common: nature did
Design us to be warriors, and to break through
Our ring, the sea, by which we are environ'd;
And we by force must fetch in what is wanting,
Or precious to us. Add to this, we are
A populous nation, and increase so fast,
That, if we by our providence are not sent
Abroad in colonies, or fall by the sword,
Not Sicily, though now it were more fruitful
Than when 't was styled the granary of great Rome,

Can yield our numerous fry bread: we must starve,
Or eat up one another.

ADORNI
The king hears
With much attention.

ASTUTIO
And seems moved with what
Bertoldo hath deliver'd.

BERTOLDO
May you live long, sir,
The king of peace, so you deny not us
The glory of the war; let not our nerves
Shrink up with sloth, nor, for want of employment,
Make younger brothers thieves: it is their swords, sir,
Must sow and reap their harvest. If examples
May move you more than arguments, look on England,
The empress of the European isles,
And unto whom alone ours yields precedence:
When did she flourish so, as when she was
The mistress of the ocean, her navies
Putting a girdle round about the world?
When the Iberian quaked, her worthies named;
And the fair flower-de-luce grew pale, set by
The red rose and the white? Let not our armour
Hung up, or our unrigg'd armada, make us
Ridiculous to the late poor snakes our neighbours,
Warm'd in our bosoms, and to whom again
We may be terrible. Rouse us, sir, from the sleep
Of idleness, and redeem our mortgaged honours.
Your birth, and justly, claims my father's kingdom;
But his heroic mind descends to me:
I will confirm so much.

ADORNI
In his looks he seems
To break ope Janus' temple.

ASTUTIO
How these younglings
Take fire from him!

ADORNI
It works an alteration
Upon the king.

ANTONIO
I can forbear no longer:
War, war, my sovereign!

FULGENTIO
The king appears
Resolved, and does prepare to speak.

ROBERTO
Think not
Our counsel 's built upon so weak a base,
As to be overturn'd, or shaken, with
Tempestuous winds of words. As I, my lord,
Before resolved you, I will not engage
My person in this quarrel; neither press
My subjects to maintain it: yet, to show
My rule is gentle, and that I have feeling
O' your master's sufferings, since these gallants, weary
Of the happiness of peace, desire to taste
The bitter sweets of war, we do consent
That, as adventurers and volunteers,
No way compell'd by us, they may make trial
Of their boasted valours.

BERTOLDO
We desire no more.

ROBERTO
'Tis well; and, but my grant in this, expect not
Assistance from me. Govern, as you please,
The province you make choice of; for, I vow
By all things sacred, if that thou miscarry
In this rash undertaking, I will hear it
No otherwise than as a sad disaster,
Fallen on a stranger; nor will I esteem
That man my subject, who, in thy extremes,
In purse or person aids thee. Take your fortune:
You know me; I have said it. So, my lord,
You have my absolute answer.

AMBASSADOR
My prince pays,
In me, his duty.

ROBERTO
Follow me, Fulgentio,
And you, Astutio.

[Flourish. Exeunt **ROBERTO, FULGENTIO, ASTUTIO,** and **ATTENDANTS.**

GASPARO
What a frown he threw,
At his departure, on you!

BERTOLDO
Let him keep
His smiles for his state flatterer, I care not.

ANTONIO
Shall we aboard to night?

AMBASSADOR
Your speed, my lord,
Doubles the benefit.

BERTOLDO
I have a business
Requires despatch; some two hours hence I'll meet you.

[Exeunt.

FOOTNOTES

[1] Show water,] i. e. to clear his sight. A proverbial periphrasis for a bribe, which, in Massinger's days, (though happily not since,) was found to be the only collyrium for the eyes of a courtier.—GIFFORD.

[2] Quarry,] i. e. the game sought.

[3] Trussing a point,] i. e. tying the strings that support the hose or breeches. These strings were tagged, and are therefore called points.

[4] The Malta habit.] The dress of the knights of Malta was black, having a cross of white waxed cloth on the left side of their cloak. None were admitted into the order but those who were noble both on the father and mother's side for four generations, unless they were, like Bertoldo, the natural sons of kings and princes.

[5] Or to steal a constable from a sleeping watch.] The constable was the captain of the band; this therefore was to deprive these trusty guardians of the night of their leader.—GIFFORD.

[6] Masters of dependencies.] They were a set of needy bravoes, who undertook to ascertain the authentic grounds of a quarrel, and in some cases to settle it, for the timorous or unskilful. In the punctilious days of our author, all matters relative to dueling were arranged, in set treatises, with a gravity that, in a business less serious, would be infinitely ridiculous. Troops of disbanded soldiers, or rather of such as pretended to be so, took up the "noble science of arms," and, with the use of the small sword, (then a novelty,) taught a jargon respecting the various modes of "honourable quarrelling,"

which, though seemingly calculated to baffle alike the patience and the understanding, was a fashionable object of study. The dramatic poets, faithful to the moral end of their high art, combated this contagious folly with the united powers of wit and humour; and, after a long and well-conducted struggle, succeeded in rendering it as contemptible as it was odious, and finally suppressed it altogether.—GIFFORD.

[7] A provant sword.] A plain, unornamented sword, such as the army is supplied with. Properly speaking, provant means provisions; but our old writers extend it to all the articles that make up the magazine of an army.—GIFFORD.

[8] Lachrymæ.] The first word of the title of a musical work composed by John Dowland, in the time of James the First. The full title was, "Lachrymæ; or, Seven Teares figured in seaven passionate Pavans (i. e. affecting, serious dances); with divers other Pavans, Galiards, and Almands, set forth to the Lute, Viols, or Violins, in five Parts." This work was very popular, and is frequently alluded to by the writers of our author's age.

[9] Entradas,] i. e. rents, revenues.

[10] To decline,] i. e. to divert from their course. This sense of the word is frequent in our old poets.

[11] Virtue, if not in action, is a vice; And when we move not forward, we go backward.] This is a beautiful improvement on Horace:

Paulum sepultæ distat inertiæ
Celata virtus.

The last line of the text alludes to the Latin adage Non progredi est regredi.—GIFFORD.

Enter **SIGNOR SYLLI**, walking fantastically, followed by **CAMIOLA** and **CLARINDA**.

CAMIOLA
Nay, signior, this is too much ceremony,
In my own house.

SYLLI
What's gracious abroad,
Must be in private practised.

CLARINDA
For your mirth's sake
Let him alone; he has been all this morning
In practice with a peruked gentleman-usher,

To teach him his true amble, and his postures,

[**SYLLI** walking by, and practising.

When he walks before a lady.

SYLLI
You may, madam,
Perhaps, believe that I in this use art,
To make you dote upon me, by exposing
My more than most rare features to your view:
But I, as I have ever done, deal simply.
Look not with too much contemplation on me;
If you do, you are lost.

CAMIOLA
Is 't possible?
What philters or love-powders do you use,
To force affection? I see nothing in
Your person but I dare look on, yet keep
My own poor heart still.

SYLLI
You are warn'd—be arm'd;
And do not lose the hope of such a husband,
In being too soon enamour'd.

CAMIOLA
Never fear it;
Though your best taking part, your wealth, were trebled,
I would not woo you. But since in your pity
You please to give me caution, tell me what
Temptations I must fly from.

SYLLI
The first is,
That you never hear me sing, for I'm a Syren:
If you observe, when I warble, the dogs howl,
As ravish'd with my ditties; and you will
Run mad to hear me.

CAMIOLA
I will stop my ears,
And keep my little wits.

SYLLI
Next, when I dance,
And come aloft thus, capers cast not a sheep's eye

Upon the quivering of my calf.

CAMIOLA
Proceed, sir.

SYLLI
Nor should your little ladyship be taken with
My pretty spider-fingers, nor my eyes,
That twinkle on both sides.

CAMIOLA
Was there ever such
A piece of motley[1] heard of!

[A knocking within.]

Who's that?

[Exit **CLARINDA**.]

You may spare
The catalogue of my dangers.

SYLLI
No, good madam;
I have not told you half.

CAMIOLA
Enough, good signior.—

[Re-enter **CLARINDA**.

Who is 't?

CLARINDA
The brother of the king.

SYLLI
Nay, start not.
The brother of the king! is he no more?
Were it the king himself, I'd give him leave
To speak his mind to you, for I am not jealous;
And, to assure your ladyship of so much,
I'll usher him in, and, that done—hide myself,

[Aside, and exit.

CAMIOLA

Camiola, if ever, now be constant:
This is, indeed, a suitor, whose sweet presence,
Courtship, and loving language, would have stagger'd
The chaste Penelope; and, to increase
The wonder, did not modesty forbid it,
I should ask that from him he sues to me for:
And yet my reason, like a tyrant, tells me
I must nor give nor take it.

[Re-enter **SYLLI** with **BERTOLDO**.

SYLLI
I must tell you,
You lose your labour. Yet you shall have my countenance
To parley with her, and I'll take special care
That none shall interrupt you.

BERTOLDO
You are courteous.

SYLLI
Come, wench, wilt thou hear wisdom?

CLARINDA
Yes, from you, sir.

[They walk aside.

BERTOLDO
If forcing this sweet favour from your hand,

[Kisses her hand.

Fair madam, argue me of too much boldness,
When you are pleased to understand I take
A parting kiss, if not excuse, at least
'Twill qualify the offence.

CAMIOLA
A parting kiss, sir!
What nation, envious of the happiness
Which Sicily enjoys in your sweet presence,
Can buy you from her? or what climate yield
Pleasures transcending those which you enjoy here,
Being both beloved and honour'd; the north-star
And guider of all hearts; and, to sum up
Your full account of happiness in a word,
The brother of the king?

BERTOLDO
Do you, alone,
And with an unexampled cruelty,
Enforce my absence, and deprive me of
Those blessings which you, with a polish'd phrase,
Seem to insinuate that I do possess,
And yet tax me as being guilty of
My wilful exile? What are titles to me,
Or popular suffrage, or my nearness to
The king in blood, or fruitful Sicily,
Though it confess'd no sovereign but myself,
When you, that are the essence of my being,
The anchor of my hopes, the real substance
Of my felicity, in your disdain,
Turn all to fading and deceiving shadows?

CAMIOLA
You tax me without cause.

BERTOLDO
You must confess it.
But answer love with love, and seal the contract
In the uniting of our souls, how gladly
(Though now I were in action, and assured,
Following my fortune, that plumed Victory
Would make her glorious stand upon my tent)
Would I put off my armour, in my heat
Of conquest, and, like Antony, pursue
My Cleopatra! Will you yet look on me
With an eye of favour?

CAMIOLA
Truth bear witness for me,
That, in the judgment of my soul, you are
A man so absolute, and circular,
In all those wish'd-for rarities that may take
A virgin captive, that, though at this instant
All scepter'd monarchs of our western world
Were rivals with you, and Camiola worthy
Of such a competition, you alone
Should wear the garland.

BERTOLDO
If so, what diverts
Your favour from me?

CAMIOLA

No mulct in yourself,
Or in your person, mind, or fortune.

BERTOLDO
What then?

CAMIOLA
The consciousness of mine own wants: alas! sir,
We are not parallels; but, like lines divided,
Can ne'er meet in one centre[2]. Your birth, sir,
Without addition, were an ample dowry
For one of fairer fortunes; and this shape,
Were you ignoble, far above all value:
To this so clear a mind, so furnish'd with
Harmonious faculties moulded from heaven,
That though you were Thersites in your features,
Of no descent, and Irus in your fortunes,
Ulysses-like, you'd force all eyes and ears
To love, but seen; and, when heard, wonder at
Your matchless story: but all these bound up
Together in one volume!—give me leave
With admiration to look upon them;
But not presume, in my own flattering hopes,
I may or can enjoy them. [3]

BERTOLDO
How you ruin
What you would seem to build up! I know no
Disparity between us: you're an heir,
Sprung from a noble family; fair, rich, young,
And every way my equal.

CAMIOLA
Sir, excuse me;
One aerie with proportion ne'er discloses
The eagle and the wren[4]:—tissue and frieze
In the same garment, monstrous! But suppose
That what 's in you excessive were diminish'd,
And my desert supplied; the stronger bar,
Religion, stops our entrance: you are, sir,
A knight of Malta, by your order bound
To a single life; you cannot marry me;
And, I assure myself, you are too noble
To seek me, though my frailty should consent,
In a base path.

BERTOLDO
A dispensation, lady,

Will easily absolve me.

CAMIOLA
O take heed, sir!
When what is vow'd to heaven is dispensed with,
To serve our ends on earth, a curse must follow,
And not a blessing.

BERTOLDO
Is there no hope left me?

CAMIOLA
Nor to myself, but is a neighbour to
Impossibility. True love should walk
On equal feet; in us it does not, sir:
But rest assured, excepting this, I shall be
Devoted to your service.

BERTOLDO
And this is your
Determinate sentence?

CAMIOLA
Not to be revoked.

BERTOLDO
Farewell, then, fairest cruel! all thoughts in me
Of women perish. Let the glorious light
Of noble war extinguish Love's dim taper.
That only lends me light to see my folly:
Honour, be thou my ever-living mistress,
And fond affection, as thy bond-slave, serve thee!

[Exit.

CAMIOLA
How soon my sun is set, he being absent,
Never to rise again! What a fierce battle
Is fought between my passions!

SYLLI
I perceive
He has his answer: now must I step in
To comfort her.

[Comes forward.]

You have found, I hope, sweet lady,

Some difference between a youth of my pitch,
And this bugbear Bertoldo. Despair not; I
May be in time entreated.

CAMIOLA
Be so now, to leave me.—
Lights for my chamber! O my heart!

[Exeunt.

FOOTNOTES

[1] A piece of motley,] i. e. a fool. Alluding to the parti-coloured garments worn by the domestic fool of our ancestors.—GIFFORD.

[2] We are not parallels; but, like lines divided,
Can ne'er meet in one centre.]
Not only Massinger, but many of our old writers, use parallels for radii.

[3] In the Proëme to Herbert's Travels, which were printed not long after The Maid of Honour, a similar expression is found: "Great Britaine—containes the summe and abridge of all sorts of excellencies, met here like parallels in their proper centre."

In the life of Dr. H. More (1710) there is a letter to a correspondent who had sent him a pious treatise, in which the same expression occurs, and is thus noticed by the doctor: "There is but one passage that I remember, which will afford them (the profane and atheistical rout of the age) a disingenuous satisfaction; which is in p. 489, where you say that straight lines drawn from the centre run parallel together. To a candid reader your intended sense can be no other than that they run [Greek: par allêlas], that is, by one another; which they may do, though they do not run all along equidistantly one by another, which is the mathematical sense of the word parallel."—Gent. Mag. May, 1782. The good doctor is, I think, the best critic on the subject that has yet appeared, and sufficiently explains Massinger.—GIFFORD.

[4] One aerie with proportion ne'er discloses The eagle and the wren.] Aerie is the nest of a bird of prey; disclose is to hatch: the meaning is, eagles and wrens are too disproportionate in bulk to be hatched in the same nest.—GIFFORD.

ACT II

SCENE I

The Same. A Room in the Palace

Enter **ROBERTO, FULGENTIO**, and **ASTUTIO.**

ROBERTO
Embark'd to-night, do you say?

FULGENTIO
I saw him aboard, sir.

ROBERTO
And without taking of his leave?

ASTUTIO
'Twas strange!

ROBERTO
Are we grown so contemptible?

FULGENTIO
'Tis far
From me, sir, to add fuel to your anger,
That, in your ill opinion of him, burns
Too hot already; else, I should affirm
It was a gross neglect.

ROBERTO
A wilful scorn
Of duty and allegiance; you give it
Too fair a name: but we shall think on 't. Can you
Guess what the numbers were, that follow'd him
In his desperate action?

FULGENTIO
More than you think, sir.
All ill-affected spirits in Palermo,
Or to your government or person, with
The turbulent swordmen, such whose poverty forced them
To wish a change, are gone along with him;
Creatures devoted to his undertakings,
In right or wrong: and, to express their zeal
And readiness to serve him, ere they went,
Profanely took the sacrament on their knees,
To live and die with him.

ROBERTO
O most impious!
Their loyalty to us forgot?

FULGENTIO
I fear so.

ASTUTIO
Unthankful as they are!

FULGENTIO
Yet this deserves not
One troubled thought in you, sir; with your pardon,
I hold that their remove from hence makes more
For your security than danger.

ROBERTO
True;
And, as I'll fashion it, they shall feel it too.
Astutio, you shall presently be despatch'd
With letters, writ and sign'd with our own hand,
To the duchess of Sienna, in excuse
Of our part in these forces sent against her.
You must, beside, from us take some instructions,
To be imparted, as you judge them useful,
To the general Gonzaga. Instantly
Prepare you for your journey.

ASTUTIO
With the wings
Of loyalty and duty.

[Exit.

FULGENTIO
I am bold
To put your majesty in mind—

ROBERTO
Of my promise,
And aids, to further you in your amorous project
To the fair and rich Camiola? there's my ring;
Whatever you shall say that I entreat,
Or can command by power, I will make good.

FULGENTIO
Ever your majesty's creature.

ROBERTO
Venus prove
Propitious to you!

[Exit.

FULGENTIO

All sorts to my wishes:
Bertoldo was my hindrance; he removed,
I now will court her in the conqueror's style;
"Come, see, and overcome."—Boy!

[Enter **PAGE**.

PAGE
Sir; your pleasure?

FULGENTIO
Haste to Camiola; bid her prepare
An entertainment suitable to a fortune
She could not hope for. Tell her, I vouchsafe
To honour her with a visit.

PAGE
'Tis a favour
Will make her proud.

FULGENTIO
I know it.

PAGE
I am gone, sir.

[Exit.

FULGENTIO
Entreaties fit not me; a man in grace
May challenge awe and privilege, by his place.

[Exit.

Enter **ADORNI, SYLLI**, and **CLARINDA**.

ADORNI
So melancholy, say you!

CLARINDA
Never given
To such retirement.

ADORNI
Can you guess the cause?

CLARINDA
If it hath not its birth and being from
The brave Bertoldo's absence, I confess
'Tis past my apprehension.

SYLLI
You are wide,
The whole field wide[1]. I, in my understanding,
Pity your ignorance.

ADORNI
Resolve us.

SYLLI
Know,
Here walks the cause. She dares not look upon me;
My beauties are so terrible and enchanting,
She cannot endure my sight.

ADORNI
There I believe you.

SYLLI
But the time will come, be comforted, when I will
Put off this vizor of unkindness to her,
And show an amorous and yielding face:
And, until then, though Hercules himself
Desire to see her, he had better eat
His club, than pass her threshold; for I will be
Her Cerberus, to guard her.

ADORNI
A good dog!

CLARINDA
Worth twenty porters.

[Enter **PAGE**.

PAGE
Keep you open house here?
No groom to attend a gentleman! O, I spy one.

SYLLI

He means not me, I am sure.

PAGE
You, sirrah sheep's-head,
With a face cut on a cat-stick[2], do you hear?
You, yeoman fewterer[3], conduct me to
The lady of the mansion, or my poniard
Shall disembogue thy soul.

SYLLI
O terrible! disembogue!
I talk'd of Hercules, and here is one
Bound up in decimo sexto.

PAGE
Answer, wretch.

SYLLI
Pray you, little gentleman, be not so furious:
The lady keeps her chamber.

PAGE
And we present,
Sent on an embassy to her! but here is
Her gentlewoman. Sirrah! hold my cloak,
While I take a leap at her lips: do it, and neatly;
Or, having first tripp'd up thy heels, I'll make
Thy back my footstool.

[Kisses **CLARINDA**.

SYLLI
Tamberlane in little!
Am I turn'd Turk[4]! What an office am I put to!

CLARINDA
My lady, gentle youth, is indisposed.

PAGE
Though she were dead and buried, only tell her,
The great man in the court, the brave Fulgentio,
Descends to visit her, and it will raise her
Out of the grave for joy.

[Enter **FULGENTIO**.

SYLLI
Here comes another!

The devil, I fear, in his holiday clothes.

PAGE
So soon!
My part is at an end then. Cover my shoulders;
When I grow great, thou shalt serve me.

FULGENTIO
Are you, sirrah,
An implement of the house?

[To **SYLLI**.

SYLLI
Sure he will make
A jointstool of me!

FULGENTIO
Or, if you belong [To **ADORNI**]
To the lady of the place, command her hither.

ADORNI
I do not wear her livery, yet acknowledge
A duty to her; and as little bound
To serve your peremptory will, as she is
To obey your summons. 'Twill become you, sir,
To wait her leisure; then, her pleasure known,
You may present your duty.

FULGENTIO
Duty! Slave,
I'll teach you manners.

ADORNI
I'm past learning; make not
A tumult in the house.

FULGENTIO
Shall I be braved thus?

[They draw.

CLARINDA
Help! murder!

[Enter **CAMIOLA**.

CAMIOLA

What insolence is this? Adorni, hold,
Hold, I command you.

FULGENTIO
Saucy groom!

CAMIOLA
Not so, sir;
However, in his life, he had dependence
Upon my father, he's a gentleman,
As well born as yourself. Put on your hat.

FULGENTIO
In my presence, without leave!

SYLLI
He has mine, madam.

CAMIOLA
And I must tell you, sir, and in plain language,
Howe'er your glittering outside promise gentry,
The rudeness of your carriage and behaviour
Speaks you a coarser thing.

SYLLI
She means a clown, sir;
I am her interpreter, for want of a better.

CAMIOLA
I am a queen in mine own house; nor must you
Expect an empire here.

SYLLI
Sure I must love her
Before the day, the pretty soul's so valiant.

CAMIOLA
What are you? and what would you with me?

FULGENTIO
Proud one,
When you know what I am, and what I came for,
And may, on your submission, proceed to,
You, in your reason, must repent the coarseness
Of my entertainment.

CAMIOLA
Why, fine man? what are you?

FULGENTIO
A kinsman of the king's.

CAMIOLA
I cry you mercy,
For his sake, not your own. But, grant you are so,
'Tis not impossible but a king may have
A fool to his kinsman,—no way meaning you, sir.

FULGENTIO
You have heard of Fulgentio?

CAMIOLA
Long since, sir;
A suit-broker in court. He has the worst
Report among good men I ever heard of,
For bribery and extortion: in their prayers,
Widows and orphans curse him for a canker
And caterpillar in the state. I hope,
Sir, you are not the man.

FULGENTIO
I reply not
As you deserve, being assured you know me;
Pretending ignorance of my person, only
To give me a taste of your wit: 'tis well, and courtly;
I like a sharp wit well.

SYLLI
I cannot endure it;
Nor any of the Syllis.

FULGENTIO
More; I know, too,
This harsh induction must serve as a foil
To the well-tuned observance and respect
You will hereafter pay me, being made
Familiar with my credit with the king,
And that (contain your joy) I deign to love you.

CAMIOLA
Love me! I am not rapt with it.

FULGENTIO
Hear 't again;
I love you honestly: now you admire me.

CAMIOLA
I do, indeed; it being a word so seldom
Heard from a courtier's mouth. But, pray you, deal plainly,
Since you find me simple; what might be the motives
Inducing you to leave the freedom of
A bachelor's life, on your soft neck to wear
The stubborn yoke of marriage; and, of all
The beauties in Palermo, to choose me,
Poor me? that is the main point you must treat of.

FULGENTIO
Why, I will tell you. Of a little thing
You are a pretty peat[5], indifferent fair too;
And, like a new-rigg'd ship, both tight and yare:
Besides, the quickness of your eye assures
An active spirit.

CAMIOLA
You are pleasant, sir;
Yet I presume that there was one thing in me,
Unmention'd yet, that took you more than all
Those parts you have remember'd.

FULGENTIO
What?

CAMIOLA
My wealth, sir.

FULGENTIO
You are in the right; without that, beauty is
A flower worn in the morning, at night trod on:
But beauty, youth, and fortune meeting in you,
I will vouchsafe to marry you.

CAMIOLA
You speak well;
And, in return, excuse me, sir, if I
Deliver reasons why, upon no terms,
I'll marry you: I fable not.

SYLLI
I am glad
To hear this: I began to have an ague.

FULGENTIO
Come, your wise reasons.

CAMIOLA
Such as they are, pray take them:
First, I am doubtful whether you are a man,
Since, for your shape, trimm'd up in a lady's dressing,
You might pass for a woman; for the fairness
Of your complexion, which you think will take me,
The colour, I must tell you, in a man,
Is weak and faint, and never will hold out,
If put to labour: give me the lovely brown,
A thick curl'd hair of the same die, a leg without
An artificial calf;—I suspect yours;
But let that pass.

SYLLI
She means me all this while,
For I have every one of those good parts;
O Sylli! fortunate Sylli!

CAMIOLA
You are moved, sir.

FULGENTIO
Fie! no; go on.

CAMIOLA
Then, as you are a courtier,
A graced one too, I fear you have been too forward;
And so much for your person. One word more,
And I have done.

FULGENTIO
I'll ease you of the trouble,
Coy and disdainful!

CAMIOLA
Save me, or else he'll beat me.

FULGENTIO
No, your own folly shall; and, since you put me
To my last charm, look upon this, and tremble.

[Shows the king's ring.

CAMIOLA
At the sight of a fair ring! the king's, I take it?
I have seen him wear the like: if he hath sent it,
As a favour, to me—

FULGENTIO
Yes, 'tis very likely,
His dying mother's gift, prized as his crown!
By this he does command you to be mine;
By his gift you are so:—you may yet redeem all.

CAMIOLA
You are in a wrong account still. Though the king may
Dispose of my life and goods, my mind's mine own,
And never shall be yours. The king, heaven bless him!
Is good and gracious, and will not compel
His subjects against their wills. I believe,
Forgetting it when he wash'd his hands, you stole it,
With an intent to awe me. But you are cozen'd;
I am still myself, and will be.

FULGENTIO
A proud haggard[6],
And not to be reclaim'd! which of your grooms,
Your coachman, fool, or footman, is the lover
Preferr'd before me?

CAMIOLA
You are foul-mouth'd.

FULGENTIO
Much fairer
Than thy black soul; and so I will proclaim thee.

CAMIOLA
Were I a man, thou durst not speak this.

FULGENTIO
Heaven
So prosper me, as I resolve to do it
To all men, and in every place: scorn'd by
A tit of ten-pence!

[Exeunt **FULGENTIO** and **PAGE**.

SYLLI
Now I begin to be valiant:
Nay, I will draw my sword. O for a brother[7]!
Do a friend's part; pray you, carry him the length of 't.
I give him three years and a day to match my Toledo,
And then we'll fight like dragons.

ADORNI

Pray, have patience.

CAMIOLA
I may live to have vengeance: my Bertoldo
Would not have heard this.

ADORNI
Madam,—

CAMIOLA
Pray you, spare
Your language. Prithee fool[8], and make me merry.

[To **SYLLI**.

SYLLI
That is my office ever.

ADORNI
I must do,
Not talk; this glorious gallant shall hear from me.

[Exeunt.

FOOTNOTES

[1] The whole field wide.] This expression, however signior Sylli picked it up, is a Latinism: Erras, tota via aberras.—GIFFORD.

[2] A cat-stick.] This, I believe, is what is now called a buck-stick, used by children in the game of tip-cat, or kit-cat.—GIFFORD.

[3] Fewterer,] i. e. a dog-keeper, or one who lets the dogs loose in the chase. The word is a corruption of the French vautrier, or vaultier.

[4] Tamberlane in little!
Am I turned Turk!]
Tamberlane was a proverbial term for a bully. To turn Turk, in our old dramatists, is generally used for a change of situation, occupation, mode of thought or action. The allusion, perhaps, is to the story of Tamberlane, who is said to have mounted his horse from the back of Bajazet, the Turkish emperor.—GIFFORD.

[5] Peat,] i. e. a delicate person. The modern word pet is supposed to be the same, probably from the French petit.

[6] Haggard,] i. e. a wild hawk.

[7] O for a brother,] i. e. a brother in arms, to do what he immediately requests Adorni to do for him: the expression was common at the time, and well understood by Massinger's audience.—GIFFORD.

[8] Fool,] i. e. play the fool.

Chambers shot off: a Flourish as to an Assault: after which, enter **GONZAGA, PIERIO, RODERIGO, JACOMO**, and **SOLDIERS**.

GONZAGA
Is the breach made assaultable?

PIERIO
Yes, and the moat
Fill'd up; the cannoneer hath done his parts;
We may enter six abreast.

RODERIGO
There's not a man
Dares show himself upon the wall.

JACOMO
Defeat not
The soldiers' hoped-for spoil.

PIERIO
If you, sir,
Delay the assault, and the city be given up
To your discretion, you in honour cannot
Use the extremity of war,—but, in
Compassion to them, you to us prove cruel.

JACOMO
And an enemy to yourself.

RODERIGO
A hindrance to
The brave revenge you have vow'd.

GONZAGA
Temper your heat,
And lose not, by too sudden rashness, that
Which, be but patient, will be offer'd to you.

Security ushers ruin; proud contempt
Of an enemy three parts vanquish'd, with desire
And greediness of spoil, have often wrested
A certain victory from the conqueror's gripe.
Discretion is the tutor of the war.
Valour the pupil; and, when we command
With lenity, and our direction's follow'd
With cheerfulness, a prosperous end must crown
Our works well undertaken.

RODERIGO
Ours are finish'd—

PIERIO
If we make use of fortune.

GONZAGA
Her false smiles
Deprive you of your judgments. The condition
Of our affairs exacts a double care,
And, like bifronted Janus, we must look
Backward, as forward: though a flattering calm
Bids us urge on, a sudden tempest raised,
Not feared, much less expected, in our rear,
May foully fall upon us, and distract us
To our confusion.—

[Enter a **SCOUT**, hastily.

Our scout! what brings
Thy ghastly looks, and sudden speed?

SCOUT
The assurance
Of a new enemy.

GONZAGA
This I foresaw and fear'd.
What are they, know'st thou?

SCOUT
They are, by their colours,
Sicilians, bravely mounted, and the brightness
Of their rich armours doubly gilded with
Reflection of the sun.

GONZAGA
From Sicily?—

The king in league! no war proclaim'd! 'tis foul:
But this must be prevented, not disputed.
Ha! how is this? your estridge[1] plumes, that but
Even now, like quills of porcupines, seem'd to threaten
The stars, drop at the rumour of a shower,
And, like to captive colours, sweep the earth!
Bear up; but in great dangers, greater minds
Are never proud. Shall a few loose troops, untrain'd
But in a customary ostentation,
Presented as a sacrifice to your valours,
Cause a dejection in you?

PIERIO
No dejection.

RODERIGO
However startled, where you lead we'll follow.

GONZAGA
'Tis bravely said. We will not stay their charge,
But meet them man to man, and horse to horse.
Pierio, in our absence hold our place;
And with our foot men and those sickly troops
Prevent a sally: I in mine own person,
With part of the cavallery, will bid
These hunters welcome to a bloody breakfast:—
But I lose time.

PIERIO
I'll to my charge.

[Exit.

GONZAGA
And we
To ours: I'll bring you on.

JACOMO
If we come off,
It's not amiss; if not, my state is settled.

[Exeunt. Alarum within.

FOOTNOTE

[1] Estridge,] i. e. ostrich.

The Same. The Citadel of Sienna

Enter **FERDINAND, DRUSO**, and **LIVIO**, on the Walls.

FERDINAND
No aids from Sicily! Hath hope forsook us;
And that vain comfort to affliction, pity,
By our vow'd friend denied us? we can nor live
Nor die with honour: like beasts in a toil,
We wait the leisure of the bloody hunter,
Who is not so far reconciled unto us,
As in one death to give a period
To our calamities; but in delaying
The fate we cannot fly from, starved with wants,
We die this night, to live again to-morrow,
And suffer greater torments.

DRUSO
There is not
Three days' provision for every soldier,
At an ounce of bread a day, left in the city.

LIVIO
To die the beggar's death, with hunger made
Anatomies while we live, cannot but crack
Our heart-strings with vexation.

FERDINAND
Would they would break,
Break altogether! How willingly, like Cato,
Could I tear out my bowels, rather than
Look on the conqueror's insulting face;
But that religion, and the horrid dream
To be suffer'd in the other world, denies it!

[Enter a **SOLDIER**.

What news with thee?

SOLDIER
From the turret of the fort,
By the rising clouds of dust, through which, like lightning,
The splendour of bright arms sometimes brake through,
I did descry some forces making towards us;

And, from the camp, as emulous of their glory,
The general, (for I know him by his horse,)
And bravely seconded, encounter'd them.
Their greetings were too rough for friends; their swords,
And not their tongues, exchanging courtesies.
By this the main battalias are join'd;
And, if you please to be spectators of
The horrid issue, I will bring you where,
As in a theatre, you may see their fates
In purple gore presented.

FERDINAND
Heaven, if yet thou art
Appeased for my wrong done to Aurelia,
Take pity of my miseries! Lead the way, friend.

[Exeunt.

SCENE V

The Same. A Plain Near the Camp

A long Charge; after which, a Flourish for Victory: then enter **GONZAGA, JACOMO,** and **RODERIGO,** wounded; **BERTOLDO, GASPARO,** and **ANTONIO, PRISONERS, OFFICERS** and **SOLDIERS.**

GONZAGA
We have them yet, though they cost us dear. This was
Charged home, and bravely follow'd. Be to yourselves
[To **JACOMO** and **RODERIGO**.
True mirrors to each other's worth; and, looking
With noble emulation on his wounds,

[Points to **BERTOLDO**.

The glorious livery of triumphant war,
Imagine these with equal grace appear
Upon yourselves. The bloody sweat you have suffer'd
In this laborious, nay, toilsome harvest,
Yields a rich crop of conquest; and the spoil,
Most precious balsam to a soldier's hurts,
Will ease and cure them. Let me look upon

[**GASPARO** and **ANTONIO** are brought forward.

The prisoners' faces. Oh, how much transform'd
From what they were! O Mars! were these toys fashion'd

To undergo the burthen of thy service?
The weight of their defensive armour bruised
Their weak effeminate limbs, and would have forced them,
In a hot day, without a blow to yield.

ANTONIO
This insultation shows not manly in you.

GONZAGA
To men I had forborne it; you are women,
Or, at the best, loose carpet-knights[1]. What fury
Seduced you to exchange your ease in court
For labour in the field? Perhaps you thought
To charge, through dust and blood, an armed foe,
Was but like graceful running at the ring
For a wanton mistress' glove; and the encounter,
A soft impression on her lips:—but you
Are gaudy butterflies, and I wrong myself
In parling with you.

GASPARO
Voe victis! now we prove it.

RODERIGO
But here's one fashion'd in another mould,
And made of tougher metal.

GONZAGA
True; I owe him
For this wound bravely given.

BERTOLDO
O that mountains
Were heap'd upon me, that I might expire,
A wretch no more remember'd! [Aside.

GONZAGA
Look up, sir;
To be o'ercome deserves no shame. If you
Had fallen ingloriously, or could accuse
Your want of courage in resistance, 'twere
To be lamented: but, since you perform'd
As much as could be hoped for from a man,
(Fortune his enemy,) you wrong yourself
In this dejection. I am honour'd in
My victory over you; but to have these
My prisoners, is, in my true judgment, rather
Captivity than a triumph: you shall find

Fair quarter from me, and your many wounds,
Which I hope are not mortal, with such care
Look'd to and cured, as if your nearest friend
Attended on you.

BERTOLDO
When you know me better,
You will make void this promise: can you call me
Into your memory?

GONZAGA
The brave Bertoldo!
A brother of our order! By St. John,
Our holy patron, I am more amazed,
Nay, thunderstruck with thy apostacy,
And precipice from the most solemn vows
Made unto Heaven when this, the glorious badge
Of our Redeemer, was conferred upon thee
By the great master, than if I had seen
A reprobate Jew, an atheist, Turk, or Tartar,
Baptized in our religion!

BERTOLDO
This I look'd for;
And am resolved to suffer.

GONZAGA
Fellow-soldiers,
Behold this man, and, taught by his example,
Know that 'tis safer far to play with lightning,
Than trifle in things sacred. In my rage

[Weeps.

I shed these at the funeral of his virtue,
Faith, and religion; why, I will tell you:—
He was a gentleman so train'd up and fashion'd
For noble uses, and his youth did promise
Such certainties, more than hopes, of great achievements,
As—if the Christian world had stood opposed
Against the Othoman race, to try the fortune
Of one encounter—this Bertoldo had been,
For his knowledge to direct, and matchless courage
To execute, without a rival, by
The votes of good men, chosen general;
As the prime soldier, and most deserving
Of all that wear the cross: which now, in justice,
I thus tear from him.

BERTOLDO
Let me die with it
Upon my breast.

GONZAGA
No; by this thou wert sworn,
On all occasions, as a knight, to guard
Weak ladies from oppression, and never
To draw thy sword against them; whereas thou,
In hope of gain or glory, when a princess,
And such a princess as Aurelia is,
Was dispossess'd by violence of what was
Her true inheritance, against thine oath
Hast, to thy uttermost, labour'd to uphold
Her falling enemy. But thou shalt pay
A heavy forfeiture, and learn too late,
Valour employ'd in an ill quarrel turns
To cowardice, and Virtue then puts on
Foul Vice's visor. This is that which cancels
All friendship's bands between us.—Bear them off;
I will hear no reply: and let the ransom
Of these, for they are yours, be highly rated.
In this I do but right, and let it be
Styled justice, and not wilful cruelty.

[Exeunt.

FOOTNOTE

[1] Carpet-knights.] A term of contempt very frequently used by our old writers. Carpet-knights were such as were made on occasion of public festivities, marriages, births, &c., in contradistinction to those that were created on the field of battle, after a victory. They were naturally little regarded by the latter; and, indeed, their title had long been given in scorn, to effeminate courtiers, favourites, &c.—GIFFORD.

ACT III

SCENE I

The Same. A Camp Before the Walls of Sienna

Enter **GONZAGA, ASTUTIO, RODERIGO,** and **JACOMO.**

GONZAGA
What I have done, sir, by the law of arms

I can and will make good.

ASTUTIO
I have no commission
To expostulate the act. These letters speak
The king my master's love to you, and his
Vow'd service to the duchess, on whose person
I am to give attendance.

GONZAGA
At this instant,
She's at Fienza: you may spare the trouble
Of riding thither: I have advertised her
Of our success, and on what humble terms
Sienna stands: though presently I can
Possess it, I defer it, that she may
Enter her own, and, as she please, dispose of
The prisoners and the spoil.

ASTUTIO
I thank you, sir.
In the mean time, if I may have your licence,
I have a nephew, and one once my ward,
For whose liberties and ransoms I would gladly
Make composition.

GONZAGA
They are, as I take it,
Call'd Gasparo and Antonio.

ASTUTIO
The same, sir.

GONZAGA
For them, you must treat with these; but, for Bertoldo,
He is mine own: if the king will ransom him,
He pays down fifty thousand crowns; if not,
He lives and dies my slave.

ASTUTIO
Pray you, a word: [Aside to **GONZAGA**.
The king will rather thank you to detain him,
Than give one crown to free him.

GONZAGA
At his pleasure.
I'll send the prisoners under guard: my business
Calls me another way.

[Exit.

ASTUTIO
My service waits you.
Now, gentlemen, for this ransom, since you are not
To be brought lower, there is no evading;
I'll be your paymaster.

RODERIGO
We desire no better.

ASTUTIO
But not a word of what's agreed between us,
Till I have school'd my gallants.

JACOMO
I am dumb, sir.

[Enter a **GUARD**, with **BERTOLDO, ANTONIO,** and **GASPARO,** in irons.

BERTOLDO
And where removed now? hath the tyrant found out
Worse usage for us?

ANTONIO
Worse it cannot be.
My greyhound has fresh straw, and scraps, in his kennel;
But we have neither.

GASPARO
Did I ever think
To wear such garters on silk stockings? or
That my too curious appetite, that turn'd
At the sight of godwits, pheasant, partridge, quails,
Larks, woodcocks, calver'd salmon[1], as coarse diet,
Would leap at a mouldy crust?

ANTONIO
And go without it,
So oft as I do? Oh! how have I jeer'd
The city entertainment! A huge shoulder
Of glorious fat ram-mutton, seconded
With a pair of tame cats or conies, a crab-tart,
With a worthy loin of veal, and valiant capon,
Mortified to grow tender!—these I scorn'd,
From their plentiful horn of abundance, though invited:
But now I could carry my own stool to a tripe[2],

And call their chitterlings charity, and bless the founder.

BERTOLDO
O that I were no further sensible
Of my miseries than you are! you, like beasts,
Feel only stings of hunger, and complain not
But when you're empty: but your narrow souls
(If you have any) cannot comprehend
How insupportable the torments are,
Which a free and noble soul, made captive, suffers.
Most miserable men!—and what am I, then,
That envy you? Fetters, though made of gold,
Express base thraldom; and all delicates
Prepared by Median cooks for epicures,
When not our own, are bitter: quilts fill'd high
With gossamere and roses cannot yield
The body soft repose, the mind kept waking
With anguish and affliction.

ASTUTIO
My good lord—

BERTOLDO
This is no time nor place for flattery, sir:
Pray you, style me as I am, a wretch forsaken
Of the world, as myself.

ASTUTIO
I would it were
In me to help you.

BERTOLDO
If that you want power, sir,
Lip-comfort cannot cure me. Pray you, leave me
To mine own private thoughts.

[Walks by.

ASTUTIO [Comes forward.]
My valiant nephew!
And my more than warlike ward! I am glad to see you,
After your glorious conquests. Are these chains
Rewards for your good service? if they are,
You should wear them on your necks, since they are massy,
Like aldermen of the war.

ANTONIO
You jeer us too!

GASPARO
Good uncle, name not, as you are a man of honour,
That fatal word of war; the very sound of it
Is more dreadful than a cannon.

ANTONIO
But redeem us
From this captivity, and I'll vow hereafter
Never to wear a sword, or cut my meat
With a knife that has an edge or point; I'll starve first.

ASTUTIO
Well, have more wit hereafter: for this time
You are ransom'd.

JACOMO
Off with their irons!

RODERIGO
Do, do:
If you are ours again, you know your price.

ANTONIO
Pray you, despatch us: I shall ne'er believe
I am a free man, till I set my foot
In Sicily again, and drink Palermo,
And in Palermo too.

ASTUTIO
The wind sits fair;
You shall aboard to-night: with the rising sun
You may touch upon the coast. But take your leaves
Of the late general first.

GASPARO
I will be brief.

ANTONIO
And I. My lord, Heaven keep you!

GASPARO
Yours, to use
In the way of peace; but as your soldiers, never.

ANTONIO
A pox of war! no more of war.

[Exeunt **RODERIGO, JACOMO, ANTONIO** and **GASPARO**.

BERTOLDO
Have you
Authority to loose their bonds, yet leave
The brother of your king, whose worth disdains
Comparison with such as these, in irons?
If ransom may redeem them, I have lands,
A patrimony of mine own, assign'd me
By my deceased sire, to satisfy
Whate'er can be demanded for my freedom.

ASTUTIO
I wish you had, sir; but the king, who yields
No reason for his will, in his displeasure
Hath seized on all you had; nor will Gonzaga,
Whose prisoner now you are, accept of less
Than fifty thousand crowns.

BERTOLDO
I find it now,
That misery never comes alone. But, grant
The king is yet inexorable, time
May work him to a feeling of my sufferings.
I have friends that swore their lives and fortunes were
At my devotion, and, among the rest,
Yourself, my lord, when forfeited to the law
For a foul murder, and in cold blood done,
I made your life my gift, and reconciled you
To this incensed king, and got your pardon.
—Beware ingratitude! I know you are rich,
And may pay down the sum.

ASTUTIO
I might, my lord;
But pardon me.

BERTOLDO
And will Astutio prove, then,
To please a passionate man, (the king's no more,)
False to his maker, and his reason, which
Commands more than I ask? O summer friendship,
Whose flattering leaves, that shadow'd us in our
Prosperity, with the least gust drop off
In the autumn of adversity! How like
A prison is to a grave! when dead, we are
With solemn pomp brought thither, and our heirs,
Masking their joy in false dissembled tears,

Weep o'er the herse; but earth no sooner covers
The earth brought thither, but they turn away,
With inward smiles, the dead no more remember'd:
So, enter'd in a prison—

ASTUTIO
My occasions
Command me hence, my lord.

BERTOLDO
Pray you, leave me, do;
And tell the cruel king, that I will wear
These fetters till my flesh and they are one
Incorporated substance.

[Exit **ASTUTIO.**]

In myself,
As in a glass, I'll look on human frailty,
And curse the height of royal blood; since I,
In being born near to Jove, am near his thunder[3].
Cedars once shaken with a storm, their own
Weight grubs their roots out.—Lead me where you please;
I am his, not fortune's martyr, and will die
The great example of his cruelty.

[Exit guarded.

FOOTNOTES

[1] Calver'd salmon appears to have differed but little from what is now called pickled salmon, as the directions for preparing it are—"to boil it in vinegar with oil and spices." The word is still in use, but not in the exact sense of the text. To calver fish is now a very simple process.—GIFFORD.

[2] —To a tripe,] i. e. to a tripe shop. By "carrying his own stool," he means that he would not wait for the formality of an invitation, but trust to the vender's hospitality for a meal. The singular custom of uninvited or unexpected guests bringing their seats with them is frequently noticed by the writers of Massinger's time. It is probable that the practice originated in necessity. Our ancient houses were not much encumbered with furniture, and the little which they had was moved from place to place as occasion required.—GIFFORD.

[3] In being born near to Jove, am near his thunder.] [Greek: Porrhô Dios kai te porrho keraunou].

Enter **ADORNI**.

ADORNI
He undergoes my challenge, and contemns it,
And threatens me with the late edict made
'Gainst duellists,—the altar cowards fly to.
But I, that am engaged, and nourish in me
A higher aim than fair Camiola dreams of,
Must not sit down thus. In the court I dare not
Attempt him; and in public he's so guarded,
With a herd of parasites, clients, fools, and suitors,
That a musket cannot reach him:—my designs
Admit of no delay. This is her birthday,
Which, with a fit and due solemnity,
Camiola celebrates: and on it, all such
As love or serve her usually present
A tributary duty. I'll have something
To give, if my intelligence prove true,
Shall find acceptance. I am told, near this grove
Fulgentio, every morning, makes his markets
With his petitioners; I may present him
With a sharp petition!—Ha! 'tis he: my fate
Be ever bless'd for 't!

[Enter **FULGENTIO** and **PAGE**.

FULGENTIO
Command such as wait me
Not to presume, at the least for half an hour,
To press on my retirements. Begone, sir.

[Exit **PAGE**.

Challenged! 'tis well; and by a groom! still better.
Was this shape made to fight? I have a tongue yet,
Howe'er no sword, to kill him; and what way,
This morning I'll resolve of.

[Exit.

ADORNI
I shall cross
Your resolution, or suffer for you.

[Exit following him.

Enter **CAMIOLA**, followed by **SERVANTS** with Presents; **SYLLI**, and **CLARINDA**.

SYLLI
What are all these?

CLARINDA
Servants with several presents,
And rich ones too.

1st SERVANT
With her best wishes, madam,
Of many such days to you, the lady Petula
Presents you with this fan.

2nd SERVANT
This diamond,
From your aunt Honoria.

3rd SERVANT
This piece of plate
From your uncle, old Vicentio, with your arms
Graven upon it.

CAMIOLA
Good friends, they are too
Munificent in their love and favour to me.
Out of my cabinet return such jewels
As this directs you:—[To **CLARINDA**.]—for your pains; and yours;
Nor must you be forgotten.

[Gives them money.]

Honour me
With the drinking of a health.

1st SERVANT
Gold, on my life!

2nd SERVANT
She scorns to give base silver.

3rd SERVANT

Would she had been
Born every month in the year!

1st SERVANT
Month! every day.

2nd SERVANT
Show such another maid.

3rd SERVANT
All happiness wait you!

CLARINDA
I'll see your will done.

[Exeunt **SYLLI, CLARINDA,** and **SERVANTS.**

[Enter **ADORNI** wounded.

CAMIOLA
How, Adorni wounded!

ADORNI
A scratch got in your service, else not worth
Your observation: I bring not, madam,
In honour of your birthday, antique plate,
Or pearl, for which the savage Indian dives
Into the bottom of the sea; nor diamonds
Hewn from steep rocks with danger. Such as give
To those that have, what they themselves want, aim at
A glad return with profit: yet, despise not
My offering at the altar of your favour;
Nor let the lowness of the giver lessen
The height of what's presented; since it is
A precious jewel, almost forfeited,
And dimm'd with clouds of infamy, redeem'd,
And, in its natural splendour, with addition
Restored to the true owner.

CAMIOLA
How is this?

ADORNI
Not to hold you in suspense, I bring you, madam,
Your wounded reputation cured, the sting
Of virulent malice, festering your fair name,
Pluck'd out and trod on. That proud man, that was
Denied the honour of your hand, yet durst,

With his untrue reports, revile your fame,
Compell'd by me, hath given himself the lie,
And in his own blood wrote it:—you may read
Fulgentio subscribed.

[Offering a paper.

CAMIOLA
I am amazed!

ADORNI
It does deserve it, madam. Common service
Is fit for hinds, and the reward proportion'd
To their conditions: therefore, look not on me
As a follower of your father's fortunes, or
One that subsists on yours:—you frown! my service
Merits not this aspéct.

CAMIOLA
Which of my favours,
I might say bounties, hath begot and nourish'd
This more than rude presumption? Since you had
An itch to try your desperate valour, wherefore
Went you not to the war? Couldst thou suppose
My innocence could ever fall so low
As to have need of thy rash sword to guard it
Against malicious slander? O how much
Those ladies are deceived and cheated, when
The clearness and integrity of their actions
Do not defend themselves, and stand secure
On their own bases! Such as in a colour
Of seeming service give protection to them,
Betray their own strengths. Malice scorn'd, puts out
Itself; but argued, gives a kind of credit
To a false accusation. In this, this your
Most memorable service, you believed
You did me right; but you have wrong'd me more
In your defence of my undoubted honour,
Than false Fulgentio could.

ADORNI
I am sorry what was
So well intended is so ill received;

[Re-enter **CLARINDA**.

Yet, under your correction, you wish'd
Bertoldo had been present.

CAMIOLA
True, I did:
But he and you, sir, are not parallels,
Nor must you think yourself so.

ADORNI
I am what
You'll please to have me.

CAMIOLA
If Bertoldo had
Punish'd Fulgentio's insolence, it had shown
His love to her whom, in his judgment, he
Vouchsafed to make his wife; a height, I hope,
Which you dare not aspire to. The same actions
Suit not all men alike;—but I perceive
Repentance in your looks. For this time, leave me;
I may forgive, perhaps forget, your folly:
Conceal yourself till this storm be blown over.
You will be sought for; yet, if my estate

[Gives him her hand to kiss.

Can hinder it, shall not suffer in my service.

[Exit **ADORNI**.

This gentleman is of a noble temper;
And I too harsh, perhaps, in my reproof:
Was I not, Clarinda?

CLARINDA
I am not to censure
Your actions, madam; but there are a thousand
Ladies, and of good fame, in such a cause
Would be proud of such a servant.

CAMIOLA
It may be;

[Enter a **SERVANT**.

Let me offend in this kind. Why, uncall'd for?

SERVANT
The signiors, madam, Gasparo and Antonio,
Selected friends of the renown'd Bertoldo,

Put ashore this morning.

CAMIOLA
Without him?

SERVANT
I think so.

CAMIOLA
Never think more then.

SERVANT
They have been at court,
Kiss'd the king's hand; and, their first duties done
To him, appear ambitious to tender
To you their second service.

CAMIOLA
Wait them hither.

[Exit **SERVANT**.

Fear, do not rack me! Reason, now, if ever,
Haste with thy aids, and tell me, such a wonder
As my Bertoldo is, with such care fashion'd,
Must not, nay, cannot, in Heaven's providence

[Enter **ANTONIO** and **GASPARO**.

So soon miscarry!—pray you, forbear; ere you take
The privilege, as strangers, to salute me,
(Excuse my manners,) make me first understand
How it is with Bertoldo.

GASPARO
The relation
Will not, I fear, deserve your thanks.

ANTONIO
I wish
Some other should inform you.

CAMIOLA
Is he dead?
You see, though with some fear, I dare inquire it.

GASPARO
Dead! Would that were the worst; a debt were paid then,

Kings in their birth owe nature.

CAMIOLA
Is there aught
More terrible than death?

ANTONIO
Yes, to a spirit
Like his; cruel imprisonment, and that
Without the hope of freedom.

CAMIOLA
You abuse me[1]:
The royal king cannot, in love to virtue,
(Though all springs of affection were dried up,)
But pay his ransom.

GASPARO
When you know what 'tis,
You will think otherwise: no less will do it
Than fifty thousand crowns.

CAMIOLA
A petty sum,
The price weigh'd with the purchase: fifty thousand!
To the king 'tis nothing. He that can spare more
To his minion for a masque, cannot but ransom
Such a brother at a million. You wrong
The king's magnificence.

ANTONIO
In your opinion;
But 'tis most certain: he does not alone
In himself refuse to pay it, but forbids
All other men.

CAMIOLA
Are you sure of this?

GASPARO
You may read
The edict to that purpose, publish'd by him;
That will resolve you.

CAMIOLA
Possible! pray you, stand off.
If I do not mutter treason to myself,
My heart will break; and yet I will not curse him;

He is my king. The news you have deliver'd
Makes me weary of your company; we'll salute
When we meet next. I'll bring you to the door.
Nay, pray you, no more compliments.

GASPARO
One thing more,
And that's substantial: let your Adorni
Look to himself.

ANTONIO
The king is much incensed
Against him for Fulgentio.

CAMIOLA
As I am,
For your slowness to depart.

BOTH
Farewell, sweet lady.

[Exeunt **GASPARO** and **ANTONIO**.

CAMIOLA
O more than impious times! when not alone
Subordinate ministers of justice are
Corrupted and seduced, but kings themselves,
The greater wheels by which the lesser move,
Are broken, or disjointed! could it be, else,
A king, to sooth his politic ends, should so far
Forsake his honour, as at once to break
The adamant chains of nature and religion,
To bind up atheism[2], as a defence
To his dark counsels? Will it ever be,
That to deserve too much is dangerous,
And virtue, when too eminent, a crime?
Must she serve fortune still, or, when stripp'd of
Her gay and glorious favours, lose the beauties
Of her own natural shape? O, my Bertoldo,
Thou only sun in honour's sphere, how soon
Art thou eclipsed and darken'd! not the nearness
Of blood prevailing on the king; nor all
The benefits to the general good dispensed,
Gaining a retribution! But that
To owe a courtesy to a simple virgin
Would take from the deserving, I find in me
Some sparks of fire, which, fann'd with honour's breath,
Might rise into a flame, and in men darken

Their usurp'd splendour. Ha! my aim is high,
And, for the honour of my sex, to fall so,
Can never prove inglorious.—'Tis resolved:
Call in Adorni.

CLARINDA
I am happy in
Such an employment, madam.

[Exit.

CAMIOLA
He's a man,
I know, that at a reverent distance loves me;
And such are ever faithful. What a sea
Of melting ice I walk on! what strange censures
Am I to undergo! but good intents
Deride all future rumours.

[Re-enter **CLARINDA** with **ADORNI**.

ADORNI
I obey
Your summons, madam.

CAMIOLA
Leave the place, Clarinda;
One woman, in a secret of such weight,
Wise men may think too much:

[Exit **CLARINDA**.]

—nearer, Adorni.
I warrant it with a smile.

ADORNI
I cannot ask
Safer protection; what's your will?

CAMIOLA
To doubt
Your ready desire to serve me, or prepare you
With the repetition of former merits,
Would, in my diffidence, wrong you: but I will,
And without circumstance, in the trust that I
Impose upon you, free you from suspicion.

ADORNI

I foster none of you.

CAMIOLA
I know you do not.
You are, Adorni, by the love you owe me—

ADORNI
The surest conjuration.

CAMIOLA
Take me with you[3].—
Love born of duty; but advance no further.
You are, sir, as I said, to do me service,
To undertake a task, in which your faith,
Judgment, discretion—in a word, your all
That's good, must be engaged; nor must you study,
In the execution, but what may make
For the ends I aim at.

ADORNI
They admit no rivals.

CAMIOLA
You answer well. You have heard of Bertoldo's
Captivity, and the king's neglect; the greatness
Of his ransom; fifty thousand crowns, Adorni;
Two parts of my estate!

ADORNI
To what tends this? [Aside.

CAMIOLA
Yet I so love the gentleman, for to you
I will confess my weakness, that I purpose
Now, when he is forsaken by the king,
And his own hopes, to ransom him, and receive him
Into my bosom, as my lawful husband—
Why change you colour?

ADORNI
'Tis in wonder of
Your virtue, madam.

CAMIOLA
You must, therefore, to
Sienna for me, and pay to Gonzaga
This ransom for his liberty; you shall have
Bills of exchange along with you. Let him swear

A solemn contract to me; for you must be
My principal witness, if he should—but why
Do I entertain these jealousies? You will do this?

ADORNI
Faithfully, madam—but not live long after. [Aside.

CAMIOLA
One thing I had forgot: besides his freedom,
He may want accomodations; furnish him
According to his birth.
I'll instantly despatch you.

[Exit.

ADORNI
Was there ever
Poor lover so employ'd against himself,
To make way for his rival? I must do it,
Nay, more, I will. If loyalty can find
Recompense beyond hope or imagination,
Let it fall on me in the other world,
As a reward, for in this I dare not hope it.

[Exit.

FOOTNOTES

[1] Abuse me,] i. e. practise on my credulity with a forged tale; the word often occurs in this sense.—
GIFFORD.

[2] Atheism.] Our old writers seem to have used such words as profaneness, blasphemy, atheism, &c.
with a laxity which modern practice does not acknowledge. They applied them to any extraordinary
violation of moral or natural decorum.—GIFFORD.

[3] Take me with you.] i. e. hear me out. The expression is common in our old writers.—GIFFORD.

ACT IV

SCENE I

The Siennese. A Camp Before the Walls of Sienna

Enter **GONZAGA** and **PIERIO.**

GONZAGA
You have seized upon the citadel, and disarm'd
All that could make resistance?

PIERIO
Hunger had
Done that, before we came; nor was the soldier
Compell'd to seek for prey: the famish'd wretches,
In hope of mercy, as a sacrifice offer'd
All that was worth the taking.

GONZAGA
Where is the duke of Urbin?

PIERIO
Under guard,
As you directed.

GONZAGA
See the soldiers set
In rank and file, and, as the duchess passes,
Bid them vail their ensigns.

[Loud music. Enter **RODERIGO, JACOMO**, and **AURELIA** under a Canopy.

[**ASTUTIO** presents her with letters.

AURELIA
But for these aids from Sicily sent against us,
To blast our spring of conquest in the bud;
I cannot find, my lord ambassador,
How we should entertain 't but as a wrong,
With purpose to detain us from our own,
Howe'er the king endeavours, in his letters,
To mitigate the affront.

ASTUTIO
Your grace hereafter
May hear from me such strong assurances
Of his unlimited desires to serve you,
As will, I hope, drown in forgetfulness
The memory of what's past.

AURELIA
We shall take time
To search the depth of 't further, and proceed
As our council shall direct us.

GONZAGA
We present you
With the keys of the city; all lets are removed,
Your way is smooth and easy; at your feet
Your proudest enemy falls.

AURELIA
We thank your valours:
A victory without blood is twice achieved,
And the disposure of it, to us tender'd,
The greatest honour. Worthy captains, thanks!
My love extends itself to all.

GONZAGA
Make way there.

[A Guard drawn up; **AURELIA** passes through them. Loud music.

[Exeunt.

SCENE II

Sienna. A Room in the Prison

BERTOLDO is discovered in fetters, reading.

BERTOLDO
'Tis here determined, (great examples, arm'd
With arguments, produced to make it good,)
That neither tyrants, nor the wrested laws,
The people's frantic rage, sad exile, want,
Nor that which I endure, captivity,
Can do a wise man any injury.
Thus Seneca, when he wrote it, thought.—But then
Felicity courted him; his wealth exceeding
A private man's; happy in the embraces
Of his chaste wife Paulina; his house full
Of children, clients, servants, flattering friends,
Soothing his lip-positions; and created
Prince of the senate, by the general voice,
At his new pupil's suffrage: then, no doubt,
He held, and did believe, this. But no sooner
The prince's frowns and jealousies had thrown him
Out of security's lap, and a centurion
Had offer'd him what choice of death he pleased,
But told him, die he must; when straight the armour

Of his so boasted fortitude fell off,

[Throws away the book.

Complaining of his frailty. Can it then
Be censured womanish weakness in me, if,
Thus clogg'd with irons, and the period
To close up all calamities denied me,
Which was presented Seneca, I wish
I ne'er had being; at least, never knew
What happiness was; or argue with heaven's justice,
Tearing my locks, and, in defiance, throwing
Dust in the air? or, falling on the ground, thus
With my nails and teeth to dig a grave, or rend
The bowels of the earth, my step-mother,
And not a natural parent? or thus practise
To die, and, as I were insensible,
Believe I had no motion?

[Falls on his face.

[Enter **GONZAGA, ADORNI**, and **GAOLER**.

GONZAGA
There he is:
I'll not inquire by whom his ransom's paid,
I am satisfied that I have it; nor allege
One reason to excuse his cruel usage,
As you may interpret it: let it suffice
It was my will to have it so. He is yours now,
Dispose of him as you please.

[Exit.

ADORNI
Howe'er I hate him,
As one preferr'd before me, being a man,
He does deserve my pity. Sir!—he sleeps:—
Or he is dead?—

[kneels by him.]

—No, he breathes! Come near,
And, if 't be possible, without his feeling,
Take off his irons.—

[His irons taken off.]

—So; now leave us private.

[Exit **GAOLER**.

He does begin to stir; and, as transported
With a joyful dream, how he stares! and feels his legs,
As yet uncertain whether it can be
True or fantastical.

BERTOLDO [Rising.]
Ministers of mercy,
Mock not calamity. Ha! 'tis no vision!
Or, if it be, the happiest that ever
Appear'd to sinful flesh! Who's here? his face
Speaks him Adorni;—but some glorious angel,
Concealing its divinity in his shape,
Hath done this miracle, it being not an act
For wolfish man. Resolve me, if thou look'st for
Bent knees in adoration?

ADORNI
O forbear, sir!
I am Adorni, and the instrument
Of your deliverance; but the benefit
You owe another.

BERTOLDO
If he has a name,
As soon as spoken, 'tis writ on my heart
I am his bondman.

ADORNI
To the shame of men,
This great act is a woman's.

BERTOLDO
The whole sex
For her sake must be deified. How I wander
In my imagination, yet cannot
Guess who this phoenix should be!

ADORNI
'Tis Camiola.

BERTOLDO
Pray you, speak 't again; there's music in her name.
Once more, I pray you, sir.

ADORNI
Camiola,
The MAID OF HONOUR.

BERTOLDO
Cursed atheist that I was,
Only to doubt it could be any other;
Since she alone, in the abstract of herself,
That small, but ravishing substance, comprehends
Whatever is, or can be wish'd, in the
Idea of a woman! O what service,
Or sacrifice of duty, can I pay her,
If not to live and die her charity's slave,
Which is resolved already!

ADORNI
She expects not
Such a dominion o'er you. You must now,
Which is the sum of all that she desires,
By a solemn contract bind yourself, when she
Requires it, as a debt due for your freedom,
To marry her.

BERTOLDO
This does engage me further;
A payment! an increase of obligation.
To marry her!—'twas my nil ultra ever:
The end of my ambition. O that now
The holy man, she present, were prepared
To join our hands, but with that speed my heart
Wishes mine eyes might see her!

ADORNI
You must swear this.

BERTOLDO
False to Camiola! never.—Shall I now
Begin my vows to you?

ADORNI
I am no churchman;
Such a one must file it on record: you are free;
And, that you may appear like to yourself,
(For so she wish'd,) here's gold, with which you may
Redeem your trunks and servants, and whatever
Of late you lost. I have found out the captain
Whose spoil they were; his name is Roderigo.

BERTOLDO
I know him.

ADORNI
I have done my parts.

BERTOLDO
So much, sir,
As I am ever yours for 't. Now, methinks,
I walk in air! Divine Camiola—
But words cannot express thee: I'll build to thee
An altar in my soul, on which I'll offer
A still-increasing sacrifice of duty.

[Exit.

ADORNI
What will become of me now is apparent.
This Roman resolution of self-murder
Will not hold water at the high tribunal,
When it comes to be argued; my good Genius
Prompts me to this consideration. He
That kills himself to avoid misery, fears it,
And, at the best, shows but a bastard valour.
This life's a fort committed to my trust,
Which I must not yield up till it be forced:
Nor will I. He's not valiant that dares die,
But he that boldly bears calamity.

[Exit.

SCENE III

The Same. A State-room in the Palace

A Flourish. Enter **PIERIO, RODERIGO, JACOMO, GONZAGA, AURELIA, FERDINAND, ASTUTIO,** and **ATTENDANTS**.

AURELIA
A seat here for the duke. It is our glory
To overcome with courtesies, not rigour;
The lordly Roman, who held it the height
Of human happiness to have kings and queens
To wait by his triumphant chariot-wheels,
In his insulting pride, deprived himself
Of drawing near the nature of the gods,

Best known for such, in being merciful.
Yet, give me leave, but still with gentle language,
And with the freedom of a friend, to tell you,
To seek by force, what courtship could not win,
Was harsh, and never taught in Love's mild school.
Wise poets feign that Venus' coach is drawn
By doves and sparrows, not by bears and tigers.
I spare the application.

FERDINAND
In my fortune,
Heaven's justice hath confirm'd it; yet, great lady,
Since my offence grew from excess of love,
And not to be resisted, having paid, too,
With loss of liberty, the forfeiture
Of my presumption, in your clemency
It may find pardon.

AURELIA
You shall have just cause
To say it hath. The charge of the long siege
Defray'd, and the loss my subjects have sustain'd
Made good, since so far I must deal with caution,
You have your liberty.

FERDINAND
I could not hope for
Gentler conditions.

AURELIA
My lord Gonzaga,
Since my coming to Sienna, I've heard much of
Your prisoner, brave Bertoldo.

GONZAGA
Such an one,
Madam, I had.

ASTUTIO
And have still, sir, I hope.

GONZAGA
Your hopes deceive you. He is ransom'd, madam.

ASTUTIO
By whom, I pray you, sir?

GONZAGA

You had best inquire
Of your intelligencer: I am no informer.

ASTUTIO
I like not this. [Aside.

AURELIA
He is, as 'tis reported,
A goodly gentleman, and of noble parts;
A brother of your order.

GONZAGA
He was, madam,
Till he, against his oath, wrong'd you, a princess,
Which his religion bound him from.

AURELIA
Great minds,
For trial of their valours, oft maintain
Quarrels that are unjust, yet without malice;
And such a fair construction I make of him:
I would see that brave enemy.

GONZAGA
My duty
Commands me to seek for him.

AURELIA
Pray you do;
And bring him to our presence.

[Exit **GONZAGA**.

ASTUTIO
I must blast
His entertainment. [Aside.] May it please your excellency.
He is a man debauch'd, and, for his riots,
Cast off by the king my master; and that, I hope, is
A crime sufficient.

FERDINAND
To you, his subjects,
That like as your king likes.

AURELIA
But not to us;
We must weigh with our own scale.

[Re-enter **GONZAGA**, with **BERTOLDO** richly habited, and **ADORNI**.

This is he, sure.
How soon mine eye had found him! what a port
He bears! how well his bravery becomes him!
A prisoner! nay, a princely suitor, rather!
But I'm too sudden. [Aside.

GONZAGA
Madam, 'twas his suit,
Unsent for, to present his service to you,
Ere his departure.

AURELIA
With what majesty
He bears himself! [Aside.

ASTUTIO
The devil, I think, supplies him.
Ransom'd, and thus rich too!

AURELIA
You ill deserve

[**BERTOLDO**, kneeling, kisses her hand.

The favour of our hand—we are not well,
Give us more air.

[Descends suddenly.

GONZAGA
What sudden qualm is this?

AURELIA
—That lifted yours against me.

BERTOLDO
Thus, once more,
I sue for pardon.

AURELIA
Sure his lips are poison'd,
And through these veins force passage to my heart,
Which is already seized on. [Aside.

BERTOLDO
I wait, madam,

To know what your commands are; my designs
Exact me in another place.

AURELIA
Before
You have our licence to depart! If manners,
Civility of manners, cannot teach you
To attend our leisure, I must tell you, sir,
That you are still our prisoner; nor had you
Commission to free him.

GONZAGA
How's this, madam?

AURELIA
You were my substitute, and wanted power,
Without my warrant, to dispose of him:
I will pay back his ransom ten times over,
Rather than quit my interest.

BERTOLDO
This is
Against the law of arms.

AURELIA
But not of love. [Aside.
Why, hath your entertainment, sir, been such,
In your restraint, that, with the wings of fear,
You would fly from it?

BERTOLDO
I know no man, madam,
Enamour'd of his fetters, or delighting
In cold or hunger, or that would in reason
Prefer straw in a dungeon before
A down-bed in a palace.

AURELIA
How!—Come nearer:
Was his usage such?

GONZAGA
Yes, and it had been worse,
Had I foreseen this.

AURELIA
O such as thou, that have
No share in nature's bounties, know no pity

To such as have them. Look on him with my eyes,
And answer, then, whether this were a man
Whose cheeks of lovely fulness should be made
A prey to meagre famine? or these eyes,
Whose every glance store Cupid's emptied quiver,
To be dimm'd with tedious watching? or these lips,
These ruddy lips, of whose fresh colour cherries
And roses were but copies, should grow pale
For want of nectar? or these limbs, that bear
A burthen of more worth than is supported
By Atlas' wearied shoulders, should be cramp'd
With the weight of iron? O, I could dwell ever
On this description!

BERTOLDO
Is this in derision,
Or pity of me?

AURELIA
In your charity
Believe me innocent. Now you are my prisoner,
You shall have fairer quarter: you will shame
The place where you have been, should you now leave it,
Before you are recover'd. I'll conduct you
To more convenient lodgings, and it shall be
My care to cherish you. Repine who dare;
It is our will. You'll follow me?

BERTOLDO
To the centre,
Such a Sybilla guiding me.

[Exeunt **AURELIA, BERTOLDO,** and **ATTENDANTS.**

GONZAGA
Who speaks first?

FERDINAND
We stand as we had seen Medusa's head.

PIERIO
I know not what to think, I am so amazed.

RODERIGO
Amazed! I am thunderstruck.

JACOMO
We are enchanted,

And this is some illusion.

ADORNI
Heaven forbid!
In dark despair it shows a beam of hope:
Contain thy joy, Adorni. [Aside.

ASTUTIO
Such a princess,
And of so long experienced reservedness,
Break forth, and on the sudden, into flashes
Of more than doubted love!

GONZAGA
They come again,
Smiling, as I live!—Some fury hath possess'd her.
If I speak, I may be blasted.

[Re-enter **BERTOLDO** and **AURELIA**.

AURELIA
Let not, sir,
The violence of my passion nourish in you
An ill opinion; or, grant my carriage
Out of the road and garb of private women,
'Tis still done with decorum.

BERTOLDO
Gracious madam,
Vouchsafe a little pause; for I am so rapt
Beyond myself, that, till I have collected
My scatter'd faculties, I cannot tender
My resolution.

AURELIA
Consider of it:
I will not be long from you.

[**BERTOLDO** walks by musing.

GONZAGA
Pray you, fair lady,
If you can, in courtesy direct me to
The chaste Aurelia.

AURELIA
Are you blind? who are we?

GONZAGA
Another kind of thing. Her love was govern'd
By her discretion, and not ruled her reason:
The reverence and majesty of Juno
Shined in her looks, and, coming to the camp,
Appear'd a second Pallas. I can see
No such divinities in you: if I,
Without offence, may speak my thoughts, you are,
As 'twere, another Helen.

AURELIA
Good! ere long
You shall know me better.

GONZAGA
Why, if you are Aurelia,
How shall I dispose of the soldier?

ASTUTIO
May it please you
To hasten my despatch?

AURELIA
Prefer your suits
Unto Bertoldo; we will give him hearing,
And you'll find him your best advocate.

[Exit.

ASTUTIO
This is rare!

GONZAGA
What are we come to?

RODERIGO
Grown up in a moment
A favourite!

FERDINAND
He does take state already.

BERTOLDO
No, no; it cannot be:—yet, but Camiola,
There is no step between me and a crown.
Then my ingratitude! a sin in which
All sins are comprehended! Aid me, Virtue,
Or I am lost!

GONZAGA
May it please your excellence—
Second me, sir.

BERTOLDO
Then my so horrid oaths,
And hell-deep imprecations made against it!

ASTUTIO
The king, your brother, will thank you for the advancement
Of his affairs.

BERTOLDO
And yet who can hold out
Against such batteries as her power and greatness
Raise up against my weak defences?

GONZAGA
Sir,

[Re-enter **AURELIA**.

Do you dream waking? 'Slight, she's here again!
Walks she on woollen feet[1]!

AURELIA
You dwell too long
In your deliberation, and come
With a cripple's pace to that which you should fly to.

BERTOLDO
It is confess'd: yet why should I, to win
From you, that hazard all to my poor nothing,
By false play send you off a loser from me?
I am already too, too much engaged
To the king my brother's anger; and who knows
But that his doubts and politic fears, should you
Make me his equal, may draw war upon
Your territories? Were that breach made up,
I should with joy embrace what now I fear
To touch but with due reverence.

AURELIA
That hinderance
Is easily removed. I owe the king
For a royal visit, which I straight will pay him;
And having first reconciled you to his favour,

A dispensation shall meet with us.

BERTOLDO
I am wholly yours.

AURELIA
On this book seal it.

GONZAGA
What, hand and lip too! then the bargain's sure.—
You have no employment for me?

AURELIA
Yes, Gonzaga;
Provide a royal ship.

GONZAGA
A ship! St. John,
Whither are we bound now?

AURELIA
You shall know hereafter.
My lord, your pardon for my too much trenching
Upon your patience.

ADORNI
Camiola! [Aside to **BERTOLDO**.

AURELIA
How do you?

BERTOLDO
Indisposed; but I attend you.

[Exeunt all but **ADORNI**.

ADORNI
The heavy curse that waits on perjury
And foul ingratitude pursue thee ever!
Yet why from me this? in his breach of faith
My loyalty finds reward: what poisons him,
Proves mithridate[2] to me. I have perform'd
All she commanded, punctually; and now,
In the clear mirror of my truth, she may
Behold his falsehood. O that I had wings
To hear me to Palermo! This, once known,
Must change her love into a just disdain,
And work her to compassion of my pain.

[Exit.

FOOTNOTES

[1] Walks she on woollen feet.] The expression is classical (lanei pedes), but does not bear the classical sense. How Massinger understood it I cannot tell; perhaps, as equivalent to motion without noise.—GIFFORD.

[2] Mithridate.] An antidote. "Mithridate is one of the capital medicines of the shops, consisting of a great number of ingredients, and has its name from its inventor, Mithridates, King of Pontus."—QUINEY.

SCENE IV

Palermo. A Room in Camiola's House

Enter **SYLLI, CAMIOLA**, and **CLARINDA**, at several doors.

SYLLI
Undone! undone!—poor I, that whilome was
The top and ridge of my house, am, on the sudden,
Turn'd to the pitifullest animal
O' the lineage of the Syllis!

CAMIOLA
What's the matter?

SYLLI
The king—break, girdle, break!

CAMIOLA
Why, what of him?

SYLLI
Hearing how far you doted on my person,
Is come himself a suitor, with the awl
Of his authority to bore my nose,
And take you from me—Oh, oh, oh!

CAMIOLA
Do not roar so:
The king!

SYLLI
The king. Yet loving Sylli is not

So sorry for his own as your misfortune:
If the king should carry you, he can but make you
A queen, and what a simple thing is that
To the being my lawful spouse! the world can never
Afford you such a husband.

CAMIOLA
I believe you.
But how are you sure the king is so inclined?
Did not you dream this?

SYLLI
With these eyes I saw him
Dismiss his train, and lighting from his coach,
Whispering Fulgentio in the ear.

CAMIOLA
If so,
I guess the business.

SYLLI
Yonder they are; I dare not

[Enter **ROBERTO** and **FULGENTIO**.

Be seen, I am so desperate: if you forsake me,
Send me word, that I may provide a willow garland,
To wear when I drown myself. O Sylli, Sylli!

[Exit crying.

FULGENTIO
It will be worth your pains, sir, to observe
The constancy and bravery of her spirit.
Though great men tremble at your frowns, I dare
Hazard my head your majesty, set off
With terror, cannot fright her.

ROBERTO
May she answer
My expectation! [Aside.

FULGENTIO
There she is.

CAMIOLA
My knees thus
Bent to the earth, while my vows are sent upward

For the safety of my sovereign, pay the duty
Due for so great an honour, in this favour
Done to your humblest handmaid.

ROBERTO
You mistake me;
I come not, lady, that you may report
The king, to do you honour, made your house
(He being there) his court; but to correct
Your stubborn disobedience. A pardon
For that, could you obtain it, were well purchased
With this humility.

CAMIOLA
A pardon, sir!
Till I am conscious of an offence,
I will not wrong my innocence to beg one.
What is my crime, sir?

ROBERTO
Look on him I favour,
By you scorn'd and neglected.

CAMIOLA
Is that all, sir?

ROBERTO
No, minion; though that were too much.
How can you
Answer the setting on your desperate bravo
To murder him?

CAMIOLA
With your leave, I must not kneel, sir,
While I reply to this: but thus rise up
In my defence, and tell you, as a man,
(Since, when you are unjust, the deity,
Which you may challenge as a king, parts from you,)
'Twas never read in holy writ, or moral,
That subjects on their loyalty were obliged
To love their sovereign's vices: your grace, sir,
To such an undeserver is no virtue.

FULGENTIO
What think you now, sir?

CAMIOLA
Say you should love wine,

You being the king, and, 'cause I am your subject,
Must I be ever drunk? Tyrants, not kings,
By violence, from humble vassals force
The liberty of their souls. I could not love him;
And to compel affection, as I take it,
Is not found in your prerogative.

ROBERTO
Excellent virgin!
How I admire her confidence! [Aside.

CAMIOLA
He complains
Of wrong done him: but be no more a king,
Unless you do me right. Burn your decrees,
And of your laws and statutes make a fire
To thaw the frozen numbness of delinquents,
If he escape unpunish'd. Do your edicts
Call it death in any man that breaks into
Another's house to rob him, though of trifles;
And shall Fulgentio, your Fulgentio, live,
Who hath committed more than sacrilege,
In the pollution of my clear fame
By his malicious slanders?

ROBERTO
Have you done this?
Answer truly, on your life.

FULGENTIO
In the heat of blood,
Some such thing I reported.

ROBERTO
Out of my sight!
For I vow, if by true penitence thou win not
This injured lady to sue out thy pardon,
Thy grave is digg'd already.

FULGENTIO
By my own folly
I have made a fair hand of 't.

[Aside, and Exit.

ROBERTO
You shall know, lady,
While I wear a crown, Justice shall use her sword

To cut offenders off, though nearest to us.

CAMIOLA
Ay, now you show whose deputy you are:
If now I bathe your feet with tears, it cannot
Be censured superstition.

ROBERTO
You must rise;
Rise in our favour and protection ever.

[Kisses her.

CAMIOLA
Happy are subjects, when the prince is still
Guided by justice, not his passionate will.

[Exeunt.

Enter **CAMIOLA** and **SYLLI**.

CAMIOLA
You see how tender I am of the quiet
And peace of your affection, and what great ones
I put off in your favour.

SYLLI
You do wisely,
Exceeding wisely; and, when I have said,
I thank you for 't, be happy.

CAMIOLA
And good reason,
In having such a blessing.

SYLLI
When you have it;
But the bait is not yet ready.

[Enter **CLARINDA** hastily.

CAMIOLA
What news with thee, now?

CLARINDA
Off with that gown, 'tis mine; mine by your promise:
Signior Adorni is return'd! now upon entrance!
Off with it, off with it, madam!

CAMIOLA
Be not so hasty:
When I go to bed, 'tis thine.

SYLLI
You have my grant too;
But, do you hear, lady, though I give way to this,
You must hereafter ask my leave, before
You part with things of moment.

CAMIOLA
Very good;
When I'm yours I'll be govern'd.

SYLLI
Sweet obedience!

[Enter **ADORNI**.

CAMIOLA
You are well return'd.

ADORNI
I wish that the success
Of my service had deserved it.

CAMIOLA
Lives Bertoldo?

ADORNI
Yes, and return'd with safety.

CAMIOLA
'Tis not then
In the power of fate to add to, or take from
My perfect happiness; and yet—he should
Have made me his first visit.

ADORNI

So I think too;
But he—

SYLLI
Durst not appear, I being present;
That's his excuse, I warrant you.

CAMIOLA
Speak, where is he?
With whom? who hath deserved more from him? or
Can be of equal merit? I in this
Do not except the king.

ADORNI
He's at the palace,
With the duchess of Sienna. One coach brought them hither,
Without a third: he's very gracious with her;
You may conceive the rest.

CAMIOLA
My jealous fears
Make me to apprehend.

ADORNI
Pray you, dismiss
Signior Wisdom, and I'll make relation to you
Of the particulars.

CAMIOLA
Servant, I would have you
To haste unto the court.

SYLLI
I will outrun
A footman for your pleasure.

CAMIOLA
There observe
The duchess' train, and entertainment.

SYLLI
Fear not;
I will discover all that is of weight,
To the liveries of her pages and her footmen.
This is fit employment for me.

[Exit.

CAMIOLA
Gracious with
The duchess! sure you said so?

ADORNI
I will use
All possible brevity to inform you, madam,
Of what was trusted to me, and discharged
With faith and loyal duty.

CAMIOLA
I believe it;
You ransomed him, and supplied his wants—imagine
That is already spoken; and what vows
Of service he made to me, is apparent;
His joy of me, and wonder too, perspicuous;
Does not your story end so?

ADORNI
Would the end
Had answered the beginning!—In a word,
Ingratitude and perjury at the height
Cannot express him.

CAMIOLA
Take heed.

ADORNI
Truth is arm'd,
And can defend itself. It must out, madam:
I saw (the presence full) the amorous duchess
Kiss and embrace him; on his part accepted
With equal ardour; and their willing hands
No sooner join'd, but a remove was publish'd,
And put in execution.

CAMIOLA
The proofs are
Too pregnant. O Bertoldo!

ADORNI
He's not worth
Your sorrow, madam.

CAMIOLA
Tell me, when you saw this,
Did not you grieve, as I do now to hear it?

ADORNI
His precipice from goodness raising mine,
And serving as a foil to set my faith off,
I had little reason.

CAMIOLA
In this you confess
The malice of your disposition. As
You were a man, you stood bound to lament it;
And not, in flattery of your false hopes,
To glory in it. When good men pursue
The path mark'd out by virtue, the blest saints
With joy look on it, and seraphic angels
Clap their celestial wings in heavenly plaudits,
To see a scene of grace so well presented,
The fiends, and men made up of envy, mourning.
Whereas now, on the contrary, as far
As their divinity can partake of passion,
With me they weep, beholding a fair temple,
Built in Bertoldo's loyalty, turn'd to ashes
By the flames of his inconstancy, the damn'd
Rejoicing in the object.—'Tis not well
In you, Adorni.

ADORNI
What a temper dwells
In this rare virgin! [Aside.] Can you pity him,
That hath shown none to you?

CAMIOLA
I must not be
Cruel by his example. You, perhaps,
Expect now I should seek recovery
Of what I have lost, by tears, and with bent knees
Beg his compassion. No; my towering virtue,
From the assurance of my merit, scorns
To stoop so low. I'll take a nobler course,
And, confident in the justice of my cause,
The king his brother, and new mistress, judges,
Ravish him from her arms. You have the contract,
In which he swore to marry me?

ADORNI
'Tis here, madam.

CAMIOLA
He shall be, then, against his will, my husband;
And when I have him, I'll so use him!—Doubt not,

But that, your honesty being unquestion'd,
This writing, with your testimony, clears all.

ADORNI
And buries me in the dark mists of error.

CAMIOLA
I'll presently to court; pray you, give order
For my caroch[1].

[Exit **ADORNI**.]

My good angel help me,
In these my extremities!

[Re-enter **SYLLI**.

SYLLI
If you e'er will see brave sight,
Lose it not now. Bertoldo and the duchess
Are presently to be married: there's such pomp
And preparation!

CAMIOLA
If I marry, 'tis
This day, or never.

SYLLI
Why, with all my heart;
Though I break this, I'll keep the next oath I make,
And then it is quit.

CAMIOLA
Follow me to my cabinet;
You know my confessor, father Paulo?

SYLLI
Yes: shall he
Do the feat for us?

CAMIOLA
I will give in writing
Directions to him, and attire myself
Like a virgin bride; and something I will do,
That shall deserve men's praise and wonder too.

[Exeunt.

FOOTNOTE

[1] Caroch,] i. e. a large coach. Coaches are said to have been first brought into England in 1564, by William Booner, a Dutchman, who became coachman to Queen Elizabeth.—NARES.

SCENE II

The Same. A State-room in the Palace

Loud music. Enter **ROBERTO, BERTOLDO, AURELIA, FERDINAND, ASTUTIO, GONZAGA, RODERIGO, JACOMO, PIERIO**, a **BISHOP**, and **ATTENDANTS**.

ROBERTO
Had our division been greater, madam,
Your clemency, the wrong being done to you,
In pardon of it, like the rod of concord,
Must make a perfect union.—Once more,
With a brotherly affection, we receive you
Into our favour: let it be your study
Hereafter to deserve this blessing, far
Beyond your merit.

BERTOLDO
As the princess' grace
To me is without limit, my endeavours,
With all obsequiousness to serve her pleasures,
Shall know no bounds: nor will I, being made
Her husband, e'er forget the duty that
I owe her as a servant.

AURELIA
I expect not
But fair equality, since I well know,
If that superiority be due,
'Tis not to me. When you are made my consort,
All the prerogatives of my high birth cancell'd,
I'll practise the obedience of a wife,
And freely pay it.

GONZAGA
This done, as it is promised, may well stand for
A precedent to great women.

ROBERTO
One word more

Touching the articles.

[Enter **FULGENTIO, CAMIOLA, SYLLI**, and **ADORNI**.

FULGENTIO
In you alone
Lie all my hopes; you can or kill or save me;
But pity in you will become you better
(Though I confess injustice 'tis denied me)
Than too much rigour.

CAMIOLA
I will make your peace
As far as it lies in me; but must first
Labour to right myself.

AURELIA
Or add or alter
What you think fit; in him I have my all:
Heaven make me thankful for him!

ROBERTO
On to the temple.

CAMIOLA
Stay, royal sir; and, as you are a king,
Erect one[1] here, in doing justice to
An injured maid.

AURELIA
How's this?

BERTOLDO
O, I am blasted!

ROBERTO
I have given some proof, sweet lady, of my promptness
To do you right; you need not, therefore, doubt me;
And rest assured, that, this great work despatch'd,
You shall have audience, and satisfaction
To all you can demand.

CAMIOLA
To do me justice
Exacts your present care, and can admit
Of no delay. If, ere my cause be heard,
In favour of your brother you go on, sir,
Your sceptre cannot right me. He's the man,

The guilty man, whom I accuse; and you
Stand bound in duty, as you are supreme,
To be impartial. Since you are a judge,
As a delinquent look on him, and not
As on a brother: Justice painted blind,
Infers her ministers are obliged to hear
The cause, and truth, the judge, determine of it;
And not sway'd or by favour or affection,
By a false gloss, or wrested comment, alter
The true intent and letter of the law.

ROBERTO
Nor will I, madam.

AURELIA
You seem troubled, sir.

GONZAGA
His colour changes too.

CAMIOLA
The alteration
Grows from his guilt. The goodness of my cause
Begets such confidence in me, that I bring
No hired tongue to plead for me, that with gay
Rhetorical flourishes may palliate
That which, stripp'd naked, will appear deform'd.
I stand here mine own advocate; and my truth,
Deliver'd in the plainest language, will
Make good itself; nor will I, if the king
Give suffrage to it, but admit of you,
My greatest enemy, and this stranger prince,
To sit assistants with him.

AURELIA
I ne'er wrong'd you.

CAMIOLA
In your knowledge of the injury, I believe it;
Nor will you, in your justice, when you are
Acquainted with my interest in this man,
Which I lay claim to.

ROBERTO
Let us take our seats.
What is your title to him?

CAMIOLA

By this contract,
Seal'd solemnly before a reverend man,

[Presents a paper to the king.

I challenge him for my husband.

SYLLI
Ha! was I
Sent for the friar for this?

ROBERTO
This writing is
Authentical.

AURELIA
But, done in heat of blood,
Charm'd by her flatteries, as, no doubt, he was,
To be dispensed with.

FERDINAND
Add this, if you please,
The distance and disparity between
Their births and fortunes.

CAMIOLA
What can Innocence hope for,
When such as sit her judges are corrupted!
Disparity of birth or fortune, urge you?
Or syren charms? or, at his best, in me
Wants to deserve him? Call some few days back,
And, as he was, consider him, and you
Must grant him my inferior. Imagine
You saw him now in fetters, with his honour,
His liberty lost; with her black wings Despair
Circling his miseries, and this Gonzaga
Trampling on his afflictions; the great sum
Proposed for his redemption; the king
Forbidding payment of it; his near kinsmen,
With his protesting followers and friends,
Falling off from him; by the whole world forsaken;
Dead to all hope, and buried in the grave
Of his calamities; and then weigh duly
What she deserved, whose merits now are doubted,
That, as his better angel, in her bounties
Appear'd unto him, his great ransom paid,
His wants, and with a prodigal hand, supplied;
Whether, then, being my manumised slave,

He owed not himself to me?

AURELIA
Is this true?

ROBERTO
In his silence 'tis acknowledged.

GONZAGA
If you want
A witness to this purpose, I'll depose it.

CAMIOLA
If I have dwelt too long on my deservings
To this unthankful man, pray you pardon me;
The cause required it. And though now I add
A little, in my painting to the life
His barbarous ingratitude, to deter
Others from imitation, let it meet with
A fair interpretation. This serpent,
Frozen to numbness, was no sooner warm'd
In the bosom of my pity and compassion,
But, in return, he ruin'd his preserver,
The prints the irons had made in his flesh
Still ulcerous; but all that I had done,
My benefits, in sand or water written,
As they had never been, no more remember'd!
And on what ground, but his ambitious hopes
To gain this duchess' favour?

AURELIA
Yes; the object,
Look on it better, lady, may excuse
The change of his affection.

CAMIOLA
The object!
In what? forgive me, modesty, if I say
You look upon your form in the false glass
Of flattery and self-love, and that deceives you.
That you were a duchess, as I take it, was not
Character'd on your face; and, that not seen,
For other feature, make all these, that are
Experienced in women, judges of them,
And, if they are not parasites, they must grant,
For beauty without art, though you storm at it,
I may take the right-hand file.

GONZAGA
Well said, i' faith!
I see fair women on no terms will yield
Priority in beauty.

CAMIOLA
Down, proud heart!
Why do I rise up in defence of that,
Which, in my cherishing of it, hath undone me!
No, madam, I recant,—you are all beauty,
Goodness, and virtue; and poor I not worthy
As a foil to set you off: enjoy your conquest;
But do not tyrannize. Yet, as I am,
In my lowness, from your height you may look on me,
And, in your suffrage to me, make him know
That, though to all men else I did appear
The shame and scorn of women, he stands bound
To hold me as the masterpiece.

ROBERTO
By my life,
You have shown yourself of such an abject temper,
So poor and low-condition'd, as I grieve for
Your nearness to me.

FERDINAND
I am changed in my
Opinion of you, lady; and profess
The virtues of your mind an ample fortune
For an absolute monarch.

GONZAGA
Since you are resolved
To damn yourself, in your forsaking of
Your noble order for a woman, do it
For this. You may search through the world, and meet not
With such another phoenix.

AURELIA
On the sudden
I feel all fires of love quench'd in the water
Of my compassion.—Make your peace; you have
My free consent; for here I do disclaim
All interest in you: and, to further your
Desires, fair maid, composed of worth and honour,
The dispensation procured by me,
Freeing Bertoldo from his vow, makes way
To your embraces.

BERTOLDO
Oh, how have I stray'd,
And wilfully, out of the noble track
Mark'd me by virtue! till now, I was never
Truly a prisoner. To excuse my late
Captivity, I might allege the malice
Of Fortune; you, that conquer'd me, confessing
Courage in my defence was no way wanting.
But now I have surrender'd up my strengths
Into the power of Vice, and on my forehead
Branded, with mine own hand, in capital letters,
DISLOYAL, and INGRATEFUL. Though barr'd from
Human society, and hiss'd into
Some desert ne'er yet haunted with the curses
Of men and women, sitting as a judge
Upon my guilty self, I must confess
It justly falls upon me; and one tear,
Shed in compassion of my sufferings, more
Than I can hope for.

CAMIOLA
This compunction
For the wrong that you have done me, though you should
Fix here, and your true sorrow move no further,
Will, in respect I loved once, make these eyes
Two springs of sorrow for you.

BERTOLDO
In your pity
My cruelty shows more monstrous: yet I am not,
Though most ingrateful, grown to such a height
Of impudence, as, in my wishes only,
To ask your pardon. If, as now I fall
Prostrate before your feet, you will vouchsafe
To act your own revenge, treading upon me
As a viper eating through the bowels of
Your benefits, to whom, with liberty,
I owe my being, 'twill take from the burden
That now is insupportable.

CAMIOLA
Pray you, rise;
As I wish peace and quiet to my soul,
I do forgive you heartily: yet, excuse me,
Though I deny myself a blessing that,
By the favour of the duchess, seconded
With your submission, is offer'd to me;

Let not the reason I allege for 't grieve you,
You have been false once.—I have done: and if,
When I am married, as this day I will be,
As a perfect sign of your atonement with me,
You wish me joy, I will receive it for
Full satisfaction of all obligations
In which you stand bound to me.

BERTOLDO
I will do it,
And, what's more, in despite of sorrow, live
To see myself undone, beyond all hope
To be made up again.

SYLLI
My blood begins
To come to my heart again.

CAMIOLA
Pray you, signior Sylli,
Call in the holy friar: he's prepared
For finishing the work.

SYLLI
I knew I was
The man: heaven make me thankful!

[Exit.

ROBERTO
Who is this?

ASTUTIO
His father was the banker of Palermo,
And this the heir of his great wealth: his wisdom
Was not hereditary.

AURELIA
For my part,
I cannot guess the issue.

[Re-enter **SYLLI** with Father **PAULO**.

SYLLI
Do your duty;
And with all speed you can, you may despatch us.

PAULO

Thus, as a principal ornament to the church,
I seize her.

OMNES
How!

ROBERTO
So young, and so religious!

PAULO
She has forsook the world.

SYLLI
I shall run mad.

ROBERTO
Hence with the fool!

[**SYLLI** is thrust off.]

Proceed, sir.

PAULO
Look on this MAID OF HONOUR, now
Truly honour'd in her vow
She pays to heaven. This fair hair
(Favours for great kings to wear)
Must now be shorn; her rich array
Changed into a homely gray:
Instead of dainties, from the spring,
For wine, cold water we will bring;
And with fasting mortify
The feasts of sensuality.
Her jewels, beads; and she must look
Not in a glass, but holy book,
To teach her the ne'er-erring way
To immortality. O may
She, as she purposes to be
A child new-born to piety,
Perséver[2] in it, and good men,
With saints and angels, say, Amen!

CAMIOLA
This is the marriage! this the port to which
My vows must steer me! Fill my spreading sails
With the pure wind of your devotions for me,
That I may touch the secure haven, where
Eternal happiness keeps her residence,

Temptations to frailty never entering!
I am dead to the world, and thus dispose
Of what I leave behind me; and, dividing
My state into three parts, I thus bequeath it:
The first to the fair nunnery, to which
I dedicate the last and better part
Of my frail life; a second portion
To pious uses; and the third to thee,
Adorni, for thy true and faithful service.
And, ere I take my last farewell, with hope
To find a grant, my suit to you is, that
You would, for my sake, pardon this young man,
And to his merits love him, and no further.

ROBERTO
I thus confirm it.

[Gives his hand to **FULGENTIO**.

CAMIOLA
And, as e'er you hope, [To **BERTOLDO**.
Like me, to be made happy, I conjure you
To reassume your order; and in fighting
Bravely against the enemies of our faith,
Redeem your mortgaged honour.

GONZAGA
I restore this:

[Gives him the white cross.

Once more, brothers in arms.

BERTOLDO
I'll live and die so.

CAMIOLA
To you my pious wishes! And, to end
All differences, great sir, I beseech you
To be an arbitrator, and compound
The quarrel long continuing between
The duke and duchess.

ROBERTO
I will take it into
My special care.

CAMIOLA

I am then at rest. Now, father,
Conduct me where you please.

[Exeunt **PAULO** and **CAMIOLA**.

ROBERTO
She well deserves
Her name, the Maid of Honour! May she stand,
To all posterity, a fair example
For noble maids to imitate! Since to live
In wealth and pleasure's common, but to part with
Such poison'd baits is rare; there being nothing
Upon this stage of life to be commended,
Though well begun, till it be fully ended.

[Flourish. Exeunt.

FOOTNOTES

[1] Erect one here,] i. e. a temple.—M. MASON.

[2] Perséver.] So this word was anciently written and pronounced.—GIFFORD.

Very few materials exist for a life of Massinger beyond the entries of the Parish Register or the College Books, and a few slender intimations scattered here and there in the dedications to his plays. From these scanty sources the following brief memoir is derived.

Our author was born at Salisbury[1] in the year 1584: he was the son of Arthur Massinger, a gentleman in the service of Henry, the second Earl of Pembroke[2]. We must not suppose, from his being thus attached to the family of a nobleman, that the father of our poet was a person of inferior birth and station. In those days the word servant carried with it no sense of degradation. The great lords and officers of the court numbered inferior nobles among their followers. We read, in Cavendish's Life of Wolsey, that "my Lord Percy, the son and heir of the Earl of Northumberland, attended upon and was servitor to the lord-cardinal[3]:" and from the situation which Arthur Massinger held in the household of so high and influential a person as the Earl of Pembroke, we might be justly led to argue rather favourably than unfavourably of his family and his connexions. "There were," says Mr. Gifford, "many considerations which united to render this state of dependance respectable and even honourable. The secretaries, clerks, and assistants, of various departments, were not then, as now, nominated by the government, but left to the choice of the person who held the employment; and as no particular dwelling was officially set apart for their residence, they were entertained in the house of their principal. That communication, too, between noblemen of power and trust, both of a public and private nature, which is now committed to the post, was in those days managed by confidential servants, who were despatched from one to the other, and even to the sovereign[4];" and, indeed, the father of our poet himself was, we know, in one instance thus employed as the bearer of communications from his patron to Elizabeth. We read in The Sidney Letters[5], "Mr. Massinger is newly come up from the Earl of

Pembroke with letters to the queen for his lordship's leave to be away this St. George's Day." This was an errand which would not have been intrusted to the execution of any inconsiderable person: unimportant as the occasion may appear to us, it would not have been regarded in that light by Elizabeth; for no monarch ever exacted from the nobility, and particularly from her officers of state, a more rigid and scrupulous compliance with stated order than this princess.

With regard to the early youth of Massinger, we possess no information whatever. Mr. Gifford supposes that it might have been passed at Wilton, a seat belonging to the Earl of Pembroke, in the neighbourhood of Salisbury; but this mode of disposing of his early years rests on a very improbable conjecture. It may occasionally have happened that the child of a favourite dependant was admitted as the companion of the younger branches of the patron's family, and allowed to receive his education among them; but this was certainly not an ordinary case; and, like Cavendish, a large majority of the great man's servants and dependants "left wife and children, home and family, rest and quietness, only to serve him[6]."—Massinger was most likely educated at the grammar-school of Salisbury, where many distinguished characters have received the rudiments of their education, among whom the elegant and accomplished Addison is to be numbered. But wherever the first years of our poet's life may have been spent, and whatever may have been the nature of his education, we know that at the age of eighteen (May 14, 1602) he was entered at the university of Oxford, and became a commoner of St. Alban's Hall[7].

Massinger resided at Oxford about four years, and then abruptly left it, without taking any degree. The cause of this sudden departure is ascribed by Mr. Gifford to the death of his father, from whom his supplies were derived: but Davies relates a very different story, and asserts that the Earl of Pembroke, who had sent him to the university and maintained him there, withdrew the necessary allowance in consequence of his having misapplied the time demanded for severer studies, in the pursuit of a more attractive but less profitable description of literature. Each opinion is equally ungrounded on the basis of any substantial evidence, and rests almost entirely on the imagination of the biographer: what slight authority there is favours the latter supposition, which, perhaps, on the whole, is most consistent with the known circumstances of the case. Anthony Wood, who was born, lived, and died at Oxford; who spent his time in collecting and recording the gossip which circulated in the university respecting the characters and conduct of its more distinguished sons; and whose evidence, however indifferent it may be, is the best that can be obtained upon the subject, confirms the representation of Davies:— "Massinger," says Wood, "gave his mind more to poetry and romance, for about four years or more, than to logic and philosophy, which he ought to have done, as he was patronised to that end." This passage corroborates the account of Davies so far as to intimate that patronage was afforded to our author, and that cause of dissatisfaction was given to the patron; but it goes no farther: it does not even state to whom the poet was indebted for assistance, nor that the misapplication of his academic hours was at all resented by the friend from whom the assistance was received: but still Wood is very probably correct in his information that other than his paternal funds were depended upon for maintaining Massinger at the university; and if such was the case, there can be no question from whose hands they must have proceeded; while the simple fact of his having been totally neglected, from the time of his father's death, by the whole of the Pembroke family, till after the demise of the earl, carries with it a strong suspicion that some offence was committed on the side of the poet, and tenaciously remembered on the side of the peer. Henry, the second Earl of Pembroke, died (1601) the year before Massinger was admitted at Oxford; and William, the third earl, to whom the father of Massinger continued attached during life, is universally and justly considered one of the brightest ornaments of the courts of Elizabeth and James. He was a man of generous and liberal disposition; the distinguished patron of arts and learning; and a lover of poetry, which he himself cultivated with some degree of success. It is not probable—it is impossible—that such a man should have allowed the highly talented son of an old and faithful servant of his family to be checked in his course of study, and abandoned to maintain, through the early years of life, a single-handed contest with adversity, for the want of that pecuniary aid which he could have yielded and never missed, unless some strong and decided cause of displeasure had existed. Had Massinger been merely forced to leave the university, as Mr. Gifford supposes, because the funds necessary to maintain him there had failed with the life of his father, we impute an act of illiberality to the Earl of Pembroke which is inconsistent with the whole tenor of his life and character. From whatever source the expenses of our author's education were originally defrayed, their suddenly ceasing argues in favour of the account intimated by Wood and detailed by Davies. If his father had, during his life, supported him at the university, there must have been some reason for the earl's not continuing that support when the father of Massinger was no more; and perhaps the most honourable supposition for both parties is that which represents the earl as offended by the bent of our author's studies and pursuits. By adopting this view of the case we are saved from the painful necessity of either assuming, on the one hand, that a nobleman distinguished among the most amiable characters of his age allowed a highly gifted and meritorious young man, a natural dependant of his house, to languish in the want of that countenance and protection on which he had an hereditary claim; or, on the other hand, that Massinger had incurred the displeasure of his natural and hereditary patron by the commission of some more crying offence.

Every, even the slightest, surmise of Mr. Gifford is deserving attention and respect; but I cannot admit the supposition by which he would account for the alienation that subsisted between the Earl of Pembroke and our author. That distinguished critic has inferred, from the religious sentiments contained in The Virgin Martyr, that Massinger was a Roman catholic, and for that cause neglected by the protector of his father. But if the intimations scattered through this play and others should be received as sufficient evidence of the faith of Massinger, we must, on similar evidence—the intimations contained in Measure for Measure, for instance—conclude that the religion of Shakspeare was the same; and then we are cast back upon our old difficulty, and have to explain why William Earl of Pembroke, a celebrated patron of literary men, and of dramatists in particular, scorned to yield his notice to the catholic Massinger, while (to use the expression of Heminge and Condell) he "prosequuted" the catholic Shakspeare and "his works with so much favour[8]?" There are many reasons for believing Shakspeare to have been a member of the church of Rome; and the patronage afforded him by the Earl of Pembroke proves, that that nobleman extended his liberality to men of genius without any regard to distinctions of faith; but, on the other hand, we have no just grounds for assuming that Massinger really did hold the same opinions. The only evidence we have upon this point, that afforded by the general tone of his writings, is of a most vague and superficial description. What, in fact, can be inferred from it? We may from such a source derive very satisfactory information respecting the sentiments which would be favourably received by the audience, but very little respecting those of the author. The truth is, that though the national religion was reformed in its liturgy and articles, the feelings, prejudices, and superstitions of the people were still almost entirely catholic; and Massinger, like any other dramatic author, writing for the amusement of the people, necessarily addressed them in a language they would understand, and with sentiments that accorded with their own. Besides, as a poet, he would never carry his theological distinctions to his literary labours: Voltaire himself is catholic in his tragedies; and Massinger naturally adopted the creed which was most suitable to the purposes of poetry, and afforded the most picturesque ceremonies and romantic situations. I feel inclined, therefore, to dismiss entirely the theory suggested by Mr. Gifford, for these two reasons; first, supposing our author to have been a catholic, we have no reason for condemning the Earl of Pembroke as a bigot and a persecutor, who would close his eyes to the merits of so great an author, because his faith did not tally with his own; and, secondly, we have no sufficient grounds for supposing him to have been a catholic at all. But with regard to all such visionary conjectures, thinking is literally a waste of thought.

Whatever may have been the nature of Massinger's studies at Oxford, it is quite certain, from the general character of his works, that his time could not have been wasted there; and his literary acquirements, at the period of his leaving the university, appear to have been multifarious and extensive. He was about two-and-twenty (1606) when he arrived in London, where, as he more than once observes, he was driven by his necessities, and somewhat inclined, perhaps, by the peculiar bent of his talents, to dedicate himself to the service of the stage.

The theatre, when Massinger first took up his abode in the metropolis, must have presented attractions of all others the most calculated to excite the interest, and inspire the imagination, of a young man of sensibility, taste, and education like our poet. No art ever attained a more rapid maturity than the dramatic art in England. The people had, indeed, been long accustomed to a species of exhibition, called MIRACLES or MYSTERIES, founded on sacred subjects, and performed by the ministers of religion themselves, on the holy festivals, in or near the churches, and designed to instruct the ignorant in the leading facts of sacred history[9]. From the occasional introduction of allegorical characters, such as Faith, Death, Hope, or Sin, into these religious dramas, representations of another kind, called MORALITIES, had by degrees arisen, of which the plots were more artificial, regular, and connected, and which were entirely formed of such personifications: but the first rough draught of a regular tragedy and comedy—Lord Sackville's Gorboduc, and Still's Gammer Gurton's Needle[10]—were not produced till within the latter half of the sixteenth century, and little more than twenty years before the stage acquired its highest splendour in the productions of Shakspeare.

About the end of the sixteenth century, the attention of the public began to be more generally directed to the drama; and it throve most admirably beneath the cheering beams of popular favour. The theatrical performances which in the early part of Elizabeth's reign had been exhibited on temporary stages, erected in such halls or apartments as the actors could procure, or, more generally, in the yards of the larger inns, while the spectators surveyed them from the surrounding windows and galleries, began to find more convenient and permanent habitations. About the year 1569, a regular playhouse, under the appropriate name of The Theatre, was erected. It is supposed to have stood somewhere in Blackfriars; and, three years after the commencement of this establishment, the queen, yielding to her own inclination for such amusements, and disregarding the remonstrances of the Puritans, granted licence and authority to the servants of the Earl of Leicester ("for the recreation of her loving subjects, as for her own solace and pleasure when she should think good to see them") to exercise their occupation throughout the whole realm of England. From this time the number of theatres increased with the increasing demands of the people. Various noblemen had their respective companies of performers, who were associated as their servants, and acted under their protection; and when Massinger left Oxford, and commenced dramatic author, there were no less than seven principal theatres open in the metropolis.

With respect to the interior arrangements, there were very few points of difference between our modern theatres and those of the days of Massinger. The prices of admission, indeed, were considerably cheaper: to the boxes the entrance was a shilling; to the pit and galleries only sixpence. Sixpence also was the price paid for stools upon the stage; and these seats, as we learn from Decker's Gull's Hornbook, were particularly affected by the wits and critics of the time. The conduct of the audience was less restrained by the sense of public decorum, and smoking tobacco, playing at cards, eating and drinking, were generally prevalent among them. The hours of performance were also earlier: the play commencing at one o'clock. During the representation a flag was unfurled at the top of the theatre; and the stage, according to the universal practice of the age, was strewn with rushes; but, in all other respects, the theatres of Elizabeth and James's days seem to have borne a perfect resemblance to our own. They had their pit, where the inferior class of spectators, the groundlings, vented their clamorous censure or approbation; they had their boxes—rooms as they were called—to which the right of exclusive admission was engaged by the night, for the more affluent portion of the audience; and there were again the galleries, or scaffoldings above the boxes, for those who were content to purchase less commodious situations at a cheaper rate. On the stage, in the same manner, the appointments appear to have been nearly of the same description as at present. The curtain divided the audience from the actors, which, at the third sounding, not indeed of the bell, but of the trumpet, was drawn for the commencement of the performance. Malone, in his account of the ancient theatre, supposes that there were no moveable scenes; that a permanent elevation of about nine feet was raised at the back of the stage, from which, in many of the old plays, part of the dialogue was spoken; and that there was a private box on each side this platform. Such an arrangement would have destroyed all theatrical illusion; and it seems extraordinary that any spectators should desire to fix themselves in a station where they could have seen nothing but the backs and trains of the performers; but, as Malone himself acknowledges the spot to have been inconvenient, and that "it is not very easy to ascertain the precise situation where these boxes really were[11]", it may very reasonably be presumed, that they were not placed in the position that the historian of the English stage has supposed. As to the permanent floor, or upper stage, of which he speaks, he may or may not be correct in his statement. All that his quotations upon the subject really establish is, that in the old, as in the modern theatre, when the actor was to speak from a window, or balcony, or the walls of a fortress, the requisite ingenuity was not wanting to contrive a representation of the place. But with regard to the use of painted moveable scenery, it is not possible, from the very circumstances of the case, to believe him correct in his theory. Such a contrivance could not have escaped our ancestors. All the materials were ready to their hands. They had not to invent for themselves, but merely to adapt an old invention to that peculiar purpose; and at a time when every better-furnished apartment was adorned with tapestry; when even the rooms of the commonest taverns were hung with painted cloths; while all the materials were constantly before their eyes, we can hardly believe our forefathers to have been so deficient in ingenuity, as to have missed the simple contrivance of converting the common ornaments of their walls into the decorations of their theatres. But, in fact, the use of scenery was almost co-existent with the introduction of dramatic representations in this country. In the Chester Mysteries (1268), the most ancient and complete collection of the kind which we possess, is found the following stage direction: "Then Noe shall go into the arke with all his familye, his wife excepte. The arke must be boarded round about; and upon the boardes all the beastes and fowles, hereafter rehearsed, must be painted, that their wordes may agree with their pictures[12]." In this passage we have a clear reference to a painted scene. It is not likely that, in the lapse of three centuries, while all other arts were in a state of rapid improvement, and the art of dramatic writing, perhaps, more rapidly and successfully improved than any other, the art of theatrical decoration should have alone stood still. It is not improbable that their scenes were few; and that they were varied, as occasion might require, by the introduction of different pieces of stage furniture. Mr. Gifford, who adheres to the opinions of Malone, says, "A table with a pen and ink thrust in, signified that the stage was a counting-house; if these were withdrawn and two stools put in their place, it was then a tavern[13]." And this might be perfectly satisfactory as long as the business of the play was supposed to be passing within doors; but when it was removed to the open air, such meagre devices would no longer be sufficient to guide the imagination of the audience, and some new method must have been adopted to indicate the place of action. After giving the subject very considerable attention, I cannot help thinking that Steevens was right in rejecting Malone's theory, and concluding that the spectators were, as at the present day, assisted in following the progress of the story by means of painted moveable scenery. This opinion is confirmed by the ancient stage directions. In the folio Shakspeare, 1623, we read "Enter Brutus in his orchard; Enter Timon in the woods; Enter Timon from the cave." In Coriolanus, "Marcius follows them to the gates and is shut in." Innumerable instances of the same kind might be cited to prove that the ancient stage was not so defective in the necessary decorations as some antiquaries of great authority would represent. "It may be added," says Steevens, "that the dialogue of our old dramatists has such perpetual reference to objects supposed visible to the audience, that the want of scenery could not have failed to render many of the descriptions absurd. Banquo examines the outside of Inverness castle with such minuteness, that he distinguishes even the nests which the martens had built under the projecting part of its roof. Romeo, standing in a garden, points to the tops of fruit-trees gilded by the moon. The prologue speaker to the second part of Henry the Fourth expressly shows the spectators 'This worm-eaten hold of ragged stone,' in which Northumberland was lodged. Iachimo takes the most exact inventory of every article in Imogen's bed-chamber, from the silk and silver of which her tapestry was wrought, down to the Cupids that support her andirons. Had not the inside of the apartment, with its proper furniture, been represented, how ridiculous must the action of Iachimo have appeared! He must have stood looking out of the room for the particulars supposed to be visible within it." The works of Massinger would afford innumerable instances of a similar kind to vindicate the opinion which Steevens has asserted on the testimony of Shakspeare alone. But on this subject there is one passage which appears to me quite conclusive. Must not all the humour of the mock play in The Midsummer Night's Dream have been entirely lost, unless the audience before whom it was performed were accustomed to all the embellishments requisite to give effect to a dramatic representation, and could consequently estimate the absurdity of those shallow contrivances and mean substitutes for scenery devised by the ignorance of the clowns[14]?

In only one respect do I perceive any material difference between the mode of representation at the time of Massinger and at present: in his day, the female parts were performed by boys. This custom, which must in many cases have materially injured the illusion of the scene, was in others of considerable advantage: it furnished the stage with a succession of youths, regularly educated for the art, to fill, in every department of the drama, the characters suited to their age. When the lad had become too tall for Juliet, he had acquired the skill, and was most admirably fitted, both in age and appearance, for performing the part which Garrick considered the most difficult on the stage, because it needed "an old head upon young shoulders," the ardent and arduous character of Romeo. When the voice had "the mannish crack," that rendered the youth unfit to appear as the representative of the gentle Imogen, the stage possessed in him the very person that was wanting to do justice to the princely sentiments of Arviragus or Guiderius[15].

Such was the state of the stage when Massinger arrived in the metropolis, and dedicated his talents to its service. He joined a splendid fraternity, for Shakspeare, Jonson, Beaumont, Fletcher, Shirley, were then flourishing at the height of their reputation, and the full vigour of their genius. Massinger came among them no unworthy competitor for such honours and emoluments as the theatre could afford. Of the honours, indeed, he seems to have reaped a very fair and equitable portion; of the emoluments, the harvest was less abundant. In those days, very little pecuniary reward was to be gained by the dramatic poet, unless, as indeed was most frequently the case, he added the profession of the actor to that of the author, and recited the verses which he wrote. The distinguished performers of that time, Alleyn, Burbage, Heminge, Condell, Shakspeare, all appear to have died in independent, if not affluent, circumstances; but the remuneration obtained by the poet was most miserably curtailed. The price given at the theatre for a new play fluctuated between ten and twenty pounds; the copyright, if the piece was printed, might produce from six to ten pounds more; in addition to these sums, the dedication-fee may be reckoned, the usual amount of which was forty shillings. Our author appears to have produced about two or three plays every year. Most of them were successful; but, even with this industry and good fortune, his annual income would rarely have exceeded fifty pounds: and we cannot, therefore, feel surprised at finding him continually speaking of his necessities; or that the only existing document connected with his life should be one that represents him in a state of pecuniary embarrassment.

Among the papers of Dulwich College, the indefatigable Mr. Malone discovered the following letter tripartite, which, coming from persons of such deserved celebrity, cannot fail of interesting the reader.

"To our most loving friend, Mr. Phillip Hinchlow, esquire, these.

"Mr. Hinchlow,

"You understand our unfortunate extremitie, and I doe not thincke you so void of Christianitie but that you would throw so much money into the Thames as wee request now of you, rather than endanger so many innocent lives. You know there is xl. more, at least, to be receaved of you for the play. We desire you to lend us vl. of that, which shall be allowed to you; without which, we cannot be bayled, nor I play any more till this be dispatch'd. It will lose you xxl. ere the end of the next weeke, besides the hindrance of the next new play. Pray, sir, consider our cases with humanity, and now give us cause to acknowledge you our true freind in time of neede. Wee have entreated Mr. Davison to deliver this note, as well to witness your love as our promises, and always acknowledgement to be ever

"Your most thankfull and loving friends,
"NAT. FIELD[16]."

"The money shall be abated out of the money remayns for the play of Mr. Fletcher and ours.
"ROB. DABORNE[17]."

"I have ever found you a true loving friend to mee, and in soe small a suite, it beinge honest, I hope you will not fail us.
"PHILIP MASSINGER."

Indorsed.
"Received by mee, Robert Davison, of Mr. Hinchlow, for the use of Mr. Daboerne, Mr. Feeld, Mr. Messenger, the sum of vl.
"ROB. DAVISON[18]."

The occasion of the distress in which these three distinguished persons were involved it is not possible to fathom. We may imagine a thousand emergencies, either creditable or discreditable to the fame of the writers, with which the letter would perfectly tally; but, on such slight and vague intimations, no ingenuity could determine which was most likely to be correct. But from the document a circumstance is ascertained, which, before its discovery, had been called in question. Sir Aston Cockayne, a friend of Massinger, had asserted in a volume of poems, published in 1658, that our author had written in conjunction with Fletcher; Davies doubted this report, but the above letter establishes the fact beyond the possibility of dispute.

Massinger is known to have produced thirty-seven plays for the stage, a list of which is given at the conclusion of this memoir. Sixteen entire plays and the fragment of another, The Parliament of Love, alone are extant. No less than eleven of his productions, in manuscript, were in possession of Mr. Warburton (Somerset Herald), and destroyed with the rest of that gentleman's invaluable collection by his cook, who, ignorant of their worth, used them as waste paper for the purposes of the kitchen.

The great and various merits of the works of Massinger will be better seen in the following volumes than in any elaborate, critical dissertation. If our author be compared with the other dramatic writers of his age, we cannot long hesitate where to place him. More natural in his characters and more poetical in his diction than Jonson or Cartwright, more elevated and nervous than Fletcher, the only writers who can be supposed to contest his pre-eminence, Massinger ranks immediately under Shakspeare himself. Our poet excels, perhaps, more in the description than in the expression of passion; this may in some measure be ascribed to his attention to the fable: while his scenes are managed with consummate skill, the lighter shades of character and sentiment are lost in the tendency of each part to the catastrophe. The melody, force, and variety of his versification are always remarkable. The prevailing beauties of his productions are dignity and elegance; their predominant fault is want of passion.

Massinger's last play—which is unfortunately lost—The Anchoress of Pausilippo, was acted Jan. 26, 1640, about six weeks before his death, which happened on the 17th of March, 1640. He went to bed in good health, says Langbaine, and was found dead in the morning, in his own house on the Bankside. He was buried in the churchyard of St. Saviour's, and the comedians paid the last sad duty to his name, by attending him to the grave.

It does not appear, though every stone and every fragment of a stone has been carefully examined, that any monument or inscription of any kind marked the place where his dust was deposited. "The memorial of his mortality," says Gifford, "is given with a pathetic brevity, which accords but too well with the obscure and humble passages of his life: March 20, 1639-40, buried Philip Massinger, A STRANGER."

Such is all the information that remains to us of this distinguished poet. But though we are ignorant of every circumstance respecting him but that he lived, wrote, and died, we may yet form some idea of his personal character from the recommendatory poems prefixed to his several plays, in which, as Mr. Gifford justly observes, the language of his panegyrists, though warm, expresses an attachment apparently derived not so much from his talents as his virtues: he is their beloved, much-esteemed, dear, worthy, deserving, honoured, long-known, and long-loved friend. All the writers of his life represent him as a man of singular modesty, gentleness, candour, and affability; nor does it appear that he ever made or found an enemy.

FOOTNOTES:

[1] *The register of his birth is not to be found, but all writers of his life agree in naming this city as the place of his nativity; and their account is corroborated by the college entry, which styles him Salisburiensis.*

[2] *Dedication to The Bondman.*

[3] *Singer's edition, p. 120.*

[4] *Introduction to the Works of Massinger, p. xxxviii.*

[5] *Vol. ii. p. 933.*

[6] *Life of Wolsey, p. 517.*

[7] *The entry in the college book styles him "Phillip Massinger, Salisburiensis, generosi filius."*

[8] *Dedication to the folio edition of Shakspeare.*

[9] *Indulgences were granted to those who attended the representation of them.*

[10] *Gorboduc appeared in 1562; Gammer Gurton, in 1566.*

[11] *Reed's Shakspeare, vol. iii. p. 83, note 3.*

[12] *Reed's Shakspeare, vol. iii. p. 15.*

[13] *Gifford's Massinger, vol. i. p. 103.*

[14] *This question ought to be set at rest, methinks, by the following extract from the Book of Revels, the oldest that exists, in the office of the auditors of the imprest: "Mrs. Dane, the lynnen dealer, for canvass to paynte for houses for the players, and other properties, as monsters, great hollow trees, and such other, twenty dozen ells, 12l."—See Boswell's Shakspeare, vol. iii. p. 364, et seq.*

[15] *The first woman who appeared in a regular drama, on a public stage, played Desdemona, about the year 1660. Her name is unknown.*

[16] *Nat. Field. This celebrated actor played female parts. He was the author of two comedies: A Woman's a Weathercock, 1612, and Amends for Ladies, 1618. He also assisted Massinger in The Fatal Dowry.*

[17] *Robert Daborne was the author of two plays: The Christian turned Turk, 1612, and The poor Man's Comfort, 1655. He was a gentleman of liberal education, master of arts, and in holy orders. It is supposed that he had preferment in Ireland. A sermon by him, preached at Waterford, in 1618, is extant.*

[18] *Additions to Malone's Hist. Account of Eng. Stage, p. 488.*

PHILIP MASSINGER – A CONCISE BIBLIOGRAPHY

As would be expected many works from this time not longer exist either in part or their entirety. Further many playwrights collaborated on plays or revised them for later performances and we have used the latest position known on each of them for the bibliography below..

Solo Plays
The Maid of Honour, tragicomedy (c. 1621; printed 1632)
The Duke of Milan, tragedy (c. 1621–3; printed 1623, 1638)

The Unnatural Combat, tragedy (c. 1621–6; printed 1639)
The Bondman, tragicomedy (licensed 3 December 1623; printed 1624)
The Renegado, tragicomedy (licensed 17 April 1624; printed 1630)
The Parliament of Love, comedy (licensed 3 November 1624; MS)
A New Way to Pay Old Debts, comedy (c. 1625; printed 1632)
The Roman Actor, tragedy (licensed 11 October 1626; printed 1629)
The Great Duke of Florence, tragicomedy (licensed 5 July 1627; printed 1636)
The Picture, tragicomedy (licensed 8 June 1629; printed 1630)
The Emperor of the East, tragicomedy (licensed 11 March 1631; printed 1632)
Believe as You List, tragedy (rejected by the censor in January, but licensed 6 May 1631; MS)
The City Madam, comedy (licensed 25 May 1632; printed 1658)
The Guardian, comedy (licensed 31 October 1633; printed 1655)
The Bashful Lover, tragicomedy (licensed 9 May 1636; printed 1655)

Sir John van Olden Barnavelt, tragedy (August 1619; MS)
The Little French Lawyer, comedy (c. 1619–23; printed 1647)
A Very Woman, tragicomedy (c. 1619–22; licensed 6 June 1634; printed 1655)
The Custom of the Country, comedy (c. 1619–23; printed 1647)
The Double Marriage, tragedy (c. 1619–23; Printed 1647)
The False One, history (c. 1619–23; printed 1647)
The Prophetess, tragicomedy (licensed 14 May 1622; printed 1647)
The Sea Voyage, comedy (licensed 22 June 1622; printed 1647)
The Spanish Curate, comedy (licensed 24 October 1622; printed 1647)
The Lovers' Progress or The Wandering Lovers, tragicomedy (licensed 6 Dec 1623; rev 1634; printed 1647)
The Elder Brother, comedy (c. 1625; printed 1637).

Thierry and Theodoret, tragedy (c. 1607?; printed 1621)
The Coxcomb, comedy (1608–10; printed 1647)
Beggars' Bush, comedy (c. 1612–15?; revised 1622?; printed 1647)
Love's Cure, comedy (c. 1612–15?; revised 1625?; printed 1647).

The Honest Man's Fortune, tragicomedy (1613; printed 1647)
The Queen of Corinth, tragicomedy (c. 1616–18; printed 1647)
The Knight of Malta, tragicomedy (c. 1619; printed 1647).

The Fatal Dowry, tragedy (c. 1619, printed 1632); adapted by Nicholas Rowe: The Fair Penitent

The Fair Maid of the Inn, comedy (licensed 22 January 1626; printed 1647).

Rollo Duke of Normandy, or The Bloody Brother, tragedy (c. 1616–24; printed 1639).

The Virgin Martyr, tragedy (licensed 6 October 1620; printed 1622).

The Old Law, comedy (c. 1615–18; printed 1656).